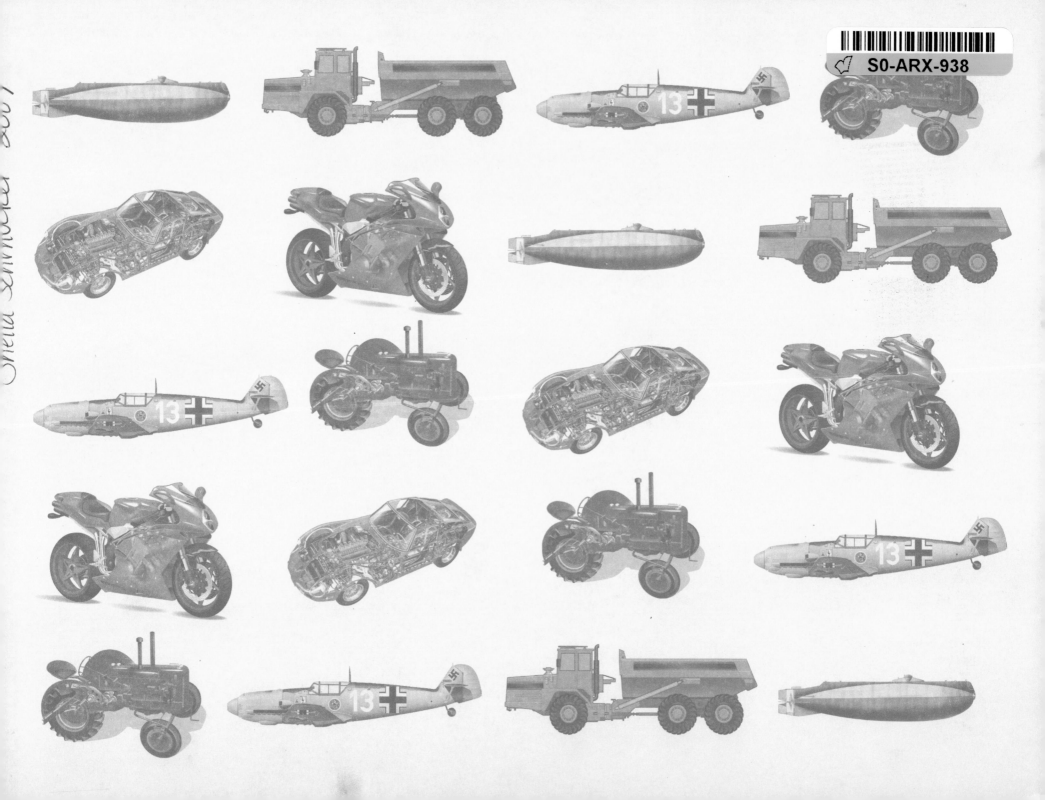

THINGS THAT GO

THINGS THAT GO

BIKES • CARS • TRACTORS • TRUCKS • HEAVY EQUIPMENT • AIRCRAFT • TRAINS

Paula Hammond

BACK**PACK**BOOKS
◦
NEW YORK

Backpack Books
122 Fifth Avenue
New York, NY 10011

ISBN 0-7607-6559-6

Printed and bound in Italy

05 06 07 08 MCH 10 9 8 7 6 5 4 3 2 1

Library of Congress Cataloging-in-Publication Data available upon request.

Editorial and design by
Amber Books Ltd
74–77 White Lion Street
London
N1 9PF
United Kingdom
www.amberbooks.co.uk

Project Editor: James Bennett
Design: Colin Hawes, Jerry Williams

Contents

CHAPTER ONE

Motorbikes

Since the invention of the bicycle in the eighteenth century, dedicated, hardworking, and downright crazy inventors have dreamed of a "motor-driven" cycle.

As early as 1869, mechanics fitted steam engines to the frames of heavy cast-iron bikes, called "bone-shakers," to produce the first self-propelled bikes. But it was an American engineer, Edward Butler, who patented the original "gasoline cycle" in 1884, powered by the new internal combustion engine.

Today, motorbikes are everywhere, from handy city mopeds to powerful touring bikes. Their speed and ability to weave in and out of heavy traffic has made them popular with everyone, from busy executives to the police. Yet the real reason everyone loves motorbikes is because they are a fun and stylish way to travel.

TRIUMPH SPEED TWIN (1938)

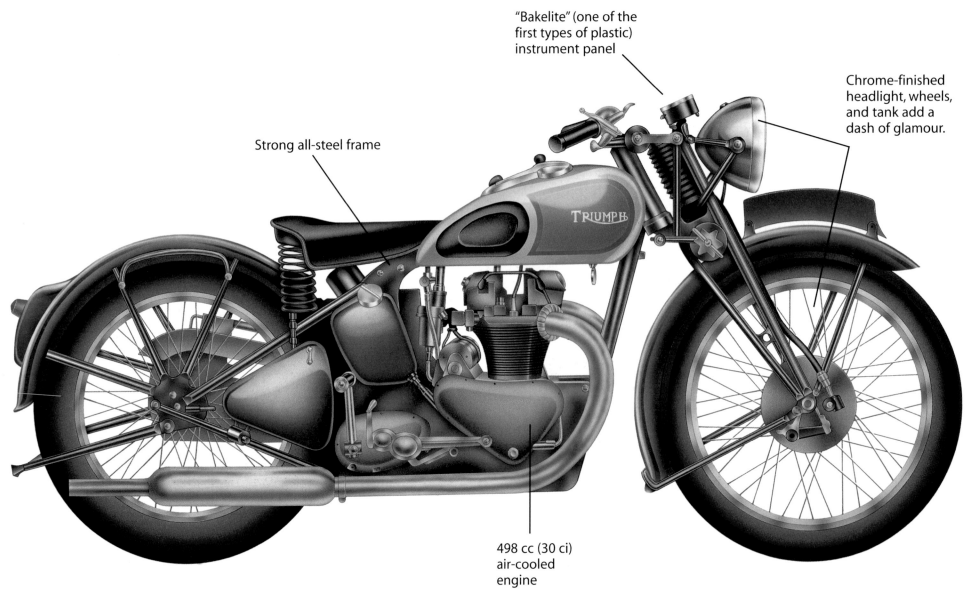

"Bakelite" (one of the first types of plastic) instrument panel

Chrome-finished headlight, wheels, and tank add a dash of glamour.

Strong all-steel frame

498 cc (30 ci) air-cooled engine

Triumph is a British company that has been making world-class motorbikes since 1885. Their masterpiece was the Speed Twin, which was first manufactured in 1937. At 353 lbs, the Speed Twin was lighter, sleeker, and faster than many other bikes of its size. It was this combination of classic style and cutting-edge design that made the Twin one of the company's most loved, desired, and copied models.

Definitions

cubic inch: A measurement of the volume of the engine's cylinders. For example, in a 30-cubic-inch twin-cylinder engine, each cylinder will have a 15-cubic-inch capacity.

cylinder: Where the fuel is burnt in a combustion engine.

Triumph Introduces the Headlight Nacelle

The speedometer tells the rider how fast they are going

The engine ignition and light switch

The ammeter measures the current going in and out of the bike's battery

ABOVE: The headlight nacelle, introduced in 1949, is an example of Triumph's fresh and stylish approach to design.

Did You Know?

The sports version of the Speed Twin set the track record at Brooklands racecourse, England, in 1939. The track closed in the same year, so the record remains unbeaten to this day!

A Triumph of Design

When Edward Turner joined Triumph in 1932, he already had a successful career in motorbike design behind him. Turner had been a designer for Ariel motorcycles, who made the popular "Red Hunter," famous for its bright red paintwork and shiny chrome exhaust pipes. Turner knew that what had worked once would work again and, in 1937, the Speed Twin (pictured above) was born. The Twin's standard color was a striking red, called amaranth, named after an imaginary flower whose color never fades. However, the Twin was more than just a pretty bike. It was also extremely light, quiet, and fast. So fast, in fact, that the London police force used the sports version, called the Tiger 100. The Tiger's top speed—118 mph—made it one of the fastest bikes of the time.

HARLEY-DAVIDSON WLA (1939–1945)

Useful maintenance
information printed
on the tank

Tommy gun and
trench-digging tools

Specially adapted
blackout lights

Large luggage rack

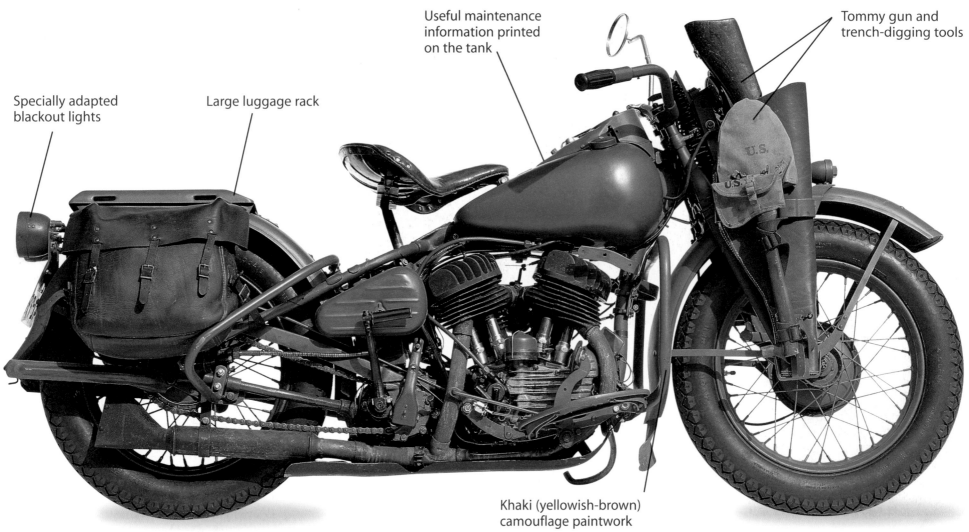

Khaki (yellowish-brown)
camouflage paintwork

Harley-Davidson motorcycles have become a universal symbol of American cool. From the throb of the V-twin engine to the laid-back riding position, these bikes are irresistible. Big, solidly built, and easy to maintain, they were also highly successful as army vehicles. During World War II, almost 68,000 WLAs were made for the armed forces. Today, it is still possible to find civilian versions of this true American classic.

Hail to the Chief!

ABOVE: A striking model in yellow, this Indian Chief motorcycle was made by the Hendee Manufacturing Company.

LEFT: The small 45 ci engine of the WLA gave it a maximum speed of only 65 mph—slower on bumpy roads!

Did You Know?

Harley-Davidson made 130 battleship-gray 44-U motorcycles for the navy. This type is the most sought after by collectors.

Fierce Competition for Harley-Davidson

Bill and Arthur Harley and Walter and Janet Davidson were the small team of friends responsible for building the very first Harley-Davidson motorcycle in 1903. Although business grew quickly, the early Harley had fierce competition from a large number of other U.S. manufacturers. Curtiss, Marsh, Royal, and Tribune all had their fans, but it was Indian that was their real rival. Indian produced motorcycles like the Indian Scout and the larger 999 cc Chief. These light, fast bikes were incredibly popular, and competition between the two companies was ferocious. When both were asked to supply motorcycles to the army during World War II, Indian designed a new bike—the Military Model 841. Harley adapted their design from an existing model, which made the WLA easier and less expensive to produce. The result was that Indian lost a lot of money and the company never really recovered. For this reason, motorcycle fans say that Indian had great designers, but Harley-Davidson was better at running a business. Indian stopped full-scale production in 1953, but even today fans argue about who really made the best bikes.

YAMAHA RD350LC YPVS (1983)

The YPVS (Yamaha Power Valve System) enables the bike to save fuel.

Front suspension using telescopic forks (see page 27)

Powerful brake disks

2-stroke, water-cooled engine

During its first 67 years in business Yamaha was famous as a maker of fine musical instruments, especially the Yamaha organ. This changed in 1955 when the company produced its first 125 cc motorbike, the YA-1. The Yamaha Motor Corporation now makes some of the world's most advanced street bikes, using technology developed on the racetrack. Yamaha's famous RD350LC YPVS ("RD" stands for "race developed") was able to reach speeds of 120 mph.

Definitions
water-cooled: When fuel is burned it reaches 4,532°F (2,500°C). This is so hot that metal engine parts must be cooled, either by water or air.

The Secret of Streamlining

When an object moves, the air or water that surrounds it slows it down. This is called "drag." The faster an object moves, the greater the drag. To reduce drag, airplanes, motorbikes, and cars have a streamlined shape. For "supersonic" (faster-than-sound) travel, the best streamlined shapes have a sharp point at the front, like rockets. For "subsonic" (slower-than-sound) travel, vehicles like bikes should have a blunt, rounded front and slightly tapered tail.

Early motorbikes weren't streamlined as most machines could only reach top speeds of around 40 mph, so there was very little drag. But when Grand Prix racing took off in the 1950s, motorbikes were much faster. Manufacturers realized that performance could be improved if they added a streamlined outer shell (known as a fairing) to the bike's frame and this is still used today. Streamlining also means that the bike doesn't have to fight against the wind, so it uses less fuel and the ride is much more comfortable.

Did You Know?

The company's founder, Torakusu Yamaha, was born 41 years before the invention of the first gasoline-engined motorbike.

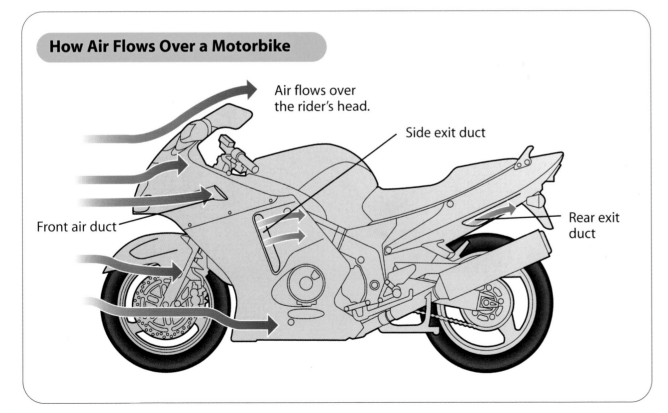

How Air Flows Over a Motorbike

Air flows over the rider's head.

Side exit duct

Front air duct

Rear exit duct

KAWASAKI GPZ900R (1984)

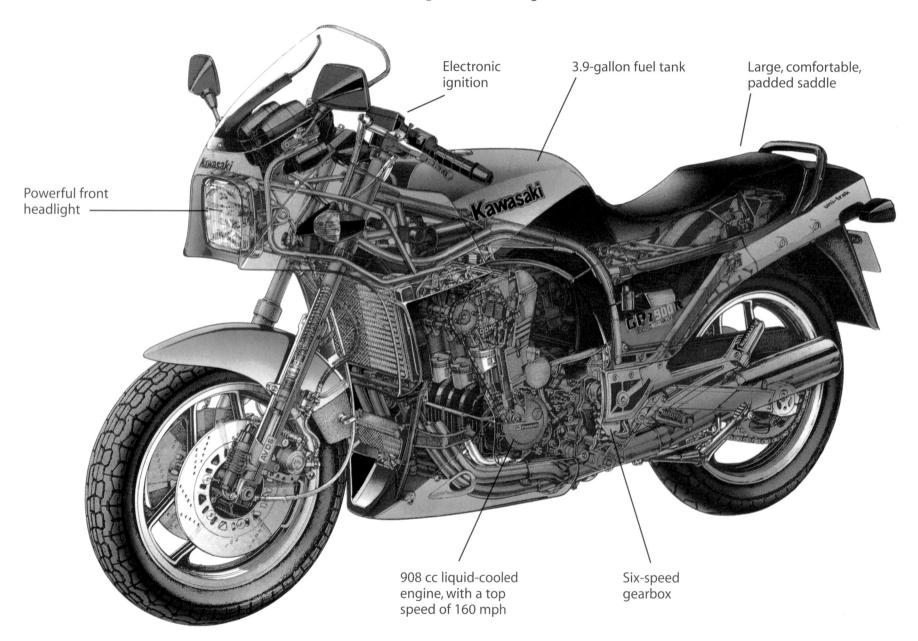

Electronic ignition

3.9-gallon fuel tank

Large, comfortable, padded saddle

Powerful front headlight

908 cc liquid-cooled engine, with a top speed of 160 mph

Six-speed gearbox

Kawasaki was better known as shipping and railroad magnates before the 1960s. But it was motorbikes such as the GPZ900R that changed all that. Called the "Ninja," it was designed to appeal to the huge American market. It was so far ahead of its time that it was produced for nine years before being replaced by a newer model. Even then, it was brought back in 1996 and 1997 due to demand.

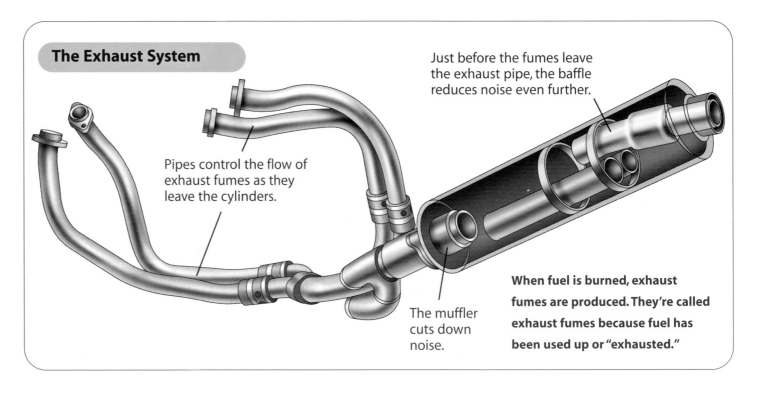

The Exhaust System

Pipes control the flow of exhaust fumes as they leave the cylinders.

Just before the fumes leave the exhaust pipe, the baffle reduces noise even further.

The muffler cuts down noise.

When fuel is burned, exhaust fumes are produced. They're called exhaust fumes because fuel has been used up or "exhausted."

What Exhausts Do

The simplest form of internal combustion engine is the "two-stroke" type. In a two-stroke engine, the piston inside the cylinder sucks in fuel and air as it moves up. This creates the first stroke. When it reaches the top of the cylinder it hits a spark plug, which ignites the fuel. The burning gases then push the piston down, which powers the engine. This is the second stroke. The gases produced are incredibly hot and under tremendous pressure. If they were allowed to come into contact with the outside air without being cooled they would expand so quickly that they'd make a loud bang. Inside the exhaust system, an ingenious arrangement of pipes stops this by cooling the gases first. Yet, exhausts do more than make bikes quieter; they keep the bike healthy by removing unwanted gases quickly and smoothly. It's possible to tell what's happening inside the engine by listening to the noise the exhaust makes. An efficient engine will have a quieter exhaust.

SUZUKI GSX-R750F (1985)

Outer fairing streamlined in racing style

Powerful front headlights

Muffler to cut down noise from exhaust

Lightweight aluminum frame

For people who love motorbikes, the ultimate bike is one that looks and feels as much like a racing bike as possible. The Suzuki GSX-R750F was just that. In fact, it was the first true "race replica" bike. Everything about it, from its lightweight racing-style fairing to its oil-cooled 749 cc engine, was based on designs tried and tested on the racetrack. The Suzuki GSX-R750F was everything that bikers had been waiting for; a fast, light, street bike that handled like a dream, and looked like a full-blooded racer.

Did You Know?

Suzuki's first engine was designed by his son, Shunzo, "just for fun." It was so successful that it secured the financial future of the company.

Silken Secrets

Silk is a fine, delicate material that Japanese artisans have been using to make elegant clothes for thousands of years. But how are this beautiful handcrafted material and the modern world of motorbike manufacturing linked? The answer is Michio Suzuki.

Suzuki was born in Hamamatsu in 1887, and by 1920 had already established a successful business building silk-weaving looms. The problem was that his looms were of such high quality that they never wore out! He desperately needed to expand his business into new areas. Suzuki's "big idea" came after World War II. At that time very little public transportation was available in Japan and he came up with the idea of designing an engine that could be added to any ordinary bicycle to produce what he called a "cyclemotor." These "Power Free" engines were a huge hit and the rest—as they say—is history! Although today Suzuki is famous for its silky-sounding motorbikes, rather than its silk looms, the company's origins are still important to it. This is why the Suzuki Motor Company celebrated its 80th anniversary in the year 2000, despite the fact that it didn't produce a motorbike until the 1950s!

ABOVE: Designed by Tansunobu Fijji, the Suzuki GSX-R750 is a cult classic.

DUCATI 916 (1994)

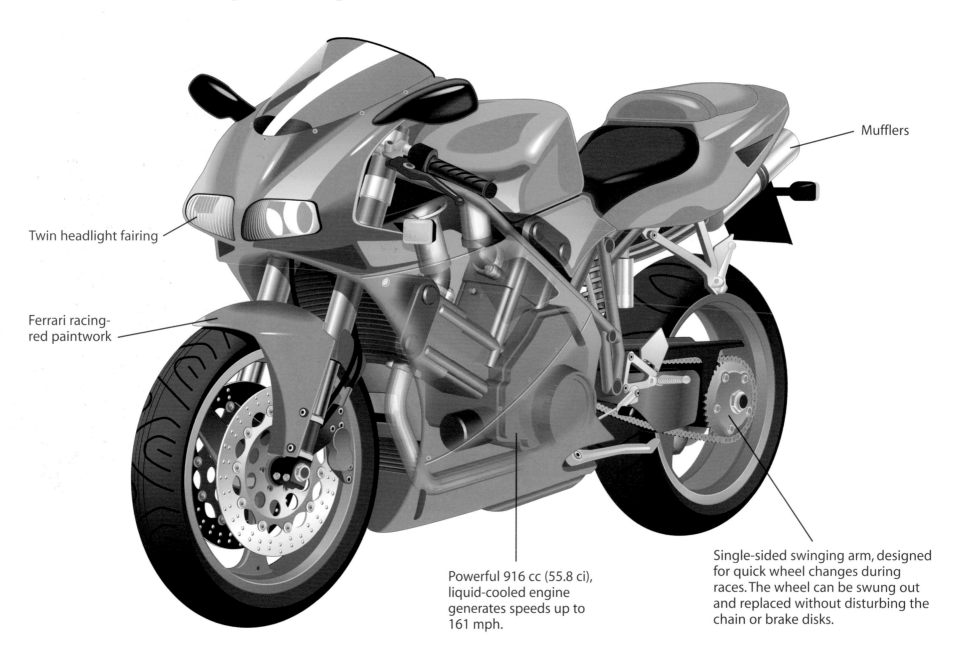

Mufflers

Twin headlight fairing

Ferrari racing-red paintwork

Powerful 916 cc (55.8 ci), liquid-cooled engine generates speeds up to 161 mph.

Single-sided swinging arm, designed for quick wheel changes during races. The wheel can be swung out and replaced without disturbing the chain or brake disks.

By the 1990s, motorbike technology had come a long way from the early engines that powered bikes like the Speed Twin (see pages 8–9). The new generation of "superbikes" was bigger, faster, and more powerful. Kawasaki, Harley-Davidson, and Triumph all made their own contribution, but it was the Ducati 916 that set the standard. Made to look and feel like a racing bike, the 916 was more than a superbike. It was *the* superbike.

Did You Know?

Ducati's first engine was a 48 cc model called "Cucciolo," which means "little puppy dog."

Mono-Shock Rear Suspension

Single-sided swinging arm

Spring

Damper unit reduces the movement of the shock absorber.

Riding in Comfort

Early bikes had a stiff frame and solid wheels—the rider felt every bump—so forms of "suspension" were quickly developed to increase comfort. These came in the form of "front forks" (see page 27), a combination of sliders and springs fixed to the front wheel to cushion the rider. Real progress came with the development of rear suspension. Bikes like the Speed Twin had fixed rear wheels, with just a spring under the seat as the rear suspension, making the ride very uncomfortable. Later machines had twin shocks (shock is short for shock absorber). These were attached from the bike's frame to each side of the rear wheel, and gave a much smoother ride. Luckily for riders, Kawasaki and Yamaha developed mono-shock (single-shock) suspension in the 1970s. This system is not only more comfortable (since there are fewer parts to vibrate), but makes the bike much easier to control.

KAWASAKI ZX-9R (1994)

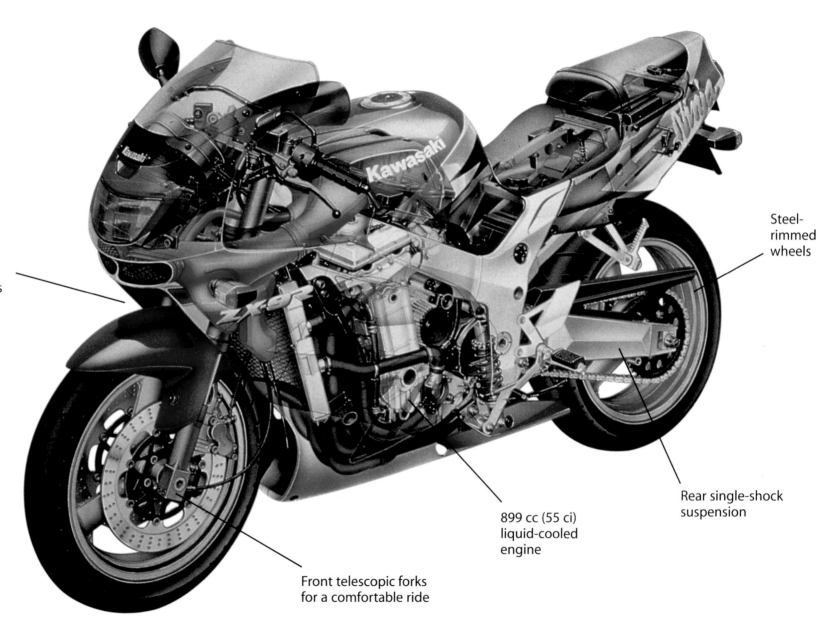

The 1994 model weighed 474 lbs, but the 1998 model was 77 lbs lighter.

Steel-rimmed wheels

Rear single-shock suspension

899 cc (55 ci) liquid-cooled engine

Front telescopic forks for a comfortable ride

Kawasaki's 1994 ZX-9R was not the high-performance bike that the company had hoped for. The machine, designed to compete with Honda's CBR900, was too heavy and handled badly at high speed. However, in 1998 they built a completely new ZX-9R. This motorbike was not only a hit, but was so successful that it was used as the basis for the ZX-12R, one of Kawasaki's fastest machines ever.

Definitions

fuel injection: In an ordinary engine, fuel and air are fed into the cylinder by a carburetor. In a fuel-injected engine, air and fuel are forced into the cylinder under high pressure. This is more efficient and gives greater power.

Kawasaki's Kings

LEFT: This is one of Kawasaki's fastest street bikes, the ZX-12R, which was first produced in the year 2000. It could reach speeds of 182 mph.

Did You Know?

Kawasaki's racing bikes have lime-green paintwork, which has earned them the nickname "Green Meanies."

Keeping Ahead of the Crowd

Since they produced their first bike in 1963, "big K," as Kawasaki is called by fans, has been responsible for some of the most important technological advances in bike manufacturing. One of Kawasaki's first big successes was the 1972 Z1, which was nicknamed the "King of the Road." This powerful 903 cc (55 ci) bike could reach 130 mph and set a standard for all future designs. From then on, Kawasaki's name became linked with high-performance "superbikes." In order to increase speed and maneuverability, Kawasaki was the first company to use fuel-injection engines as standard. They developed their own "Uni-track" single-shock suspension to give customers a smoother, safer ride. It was also the first company to introduce a design called "Forced Air Induction" as a way of increasing the power of its machines. Of the four Japanese motorbike manufacturers, Kawasaki is the smallest, but it has a big reputation for its innovative designs.

HONDA CBR 1100XX SUPER BLACKBIRD (1997)

Streamlined fairing

Ducts to direct air to the oil cooler

Computerized ignition helps to prevent theft.

Large intake duct to direct cool air onto the carburetors

Lightweight aluminum frame

The Honda CBR 1100XX Super Blackbird was named after the SR-71 Blackbird spyplane (see pages 124–125), which can reach a top speed of Mach 3.5. The Honda CBR 1100XX is a truly impressive machine. When it was first produced in 1997, its 1137 cc (69 ci) engine made it the world's fastest street bike, able to reach a breathtaking 187.5 mph.

ABOVE: Although it is designed for the road, the Blackbird is also at home on the racetrack.

Definitions
carburetor: Ensures a constant supply of air and fuel to the engine.
Mach: Mach 1 is the speed of sound, which varies with altitude but is 2,484 mph at sea level. Mach 3.5 is three and a half times the speed of sound.

The Need for Speed

Since the first motorbikes hit our streets, riders and manufacturers have been obsessed with one thing: speed! The first official bike races took place in France in 1885, and competitions such as the Paris–Vienna race proved to be hugely popular. Races gave manufacturers the chance to show potential customers what their machines could do. As race fever grew, more powerful engines were developed, along with better suspensions and gearboxes, to push machines to ever faster speeds—and hopefully leave the competition well behind.

The rate of technological development in the twentieth century was staggering. In 1907, the top speed for a racing bike at the famous Isle of Man TT (Tourist Trophy) was around 38 mph. By the 1930s, road bikes such as the Harley-Davidson WLA made 65 mph. By 1937, Ernst Henne had captured the title of "fastest on two wheels" at Brooklands racecourse, reaching a staggering 173.67 mph—a speed many of today's street bikes would struggle to beat.

Engine Power!

ABOVE: The engine casing of the CBR 1100XX was designed to be extremely durable and hard wearing.

Did You Know?

According to *The Guinness Book of Records*, the Honda Motor Company of Japan is the world's largest manufacturer of motorbikes.

MV AGUSTA F4 (1998)

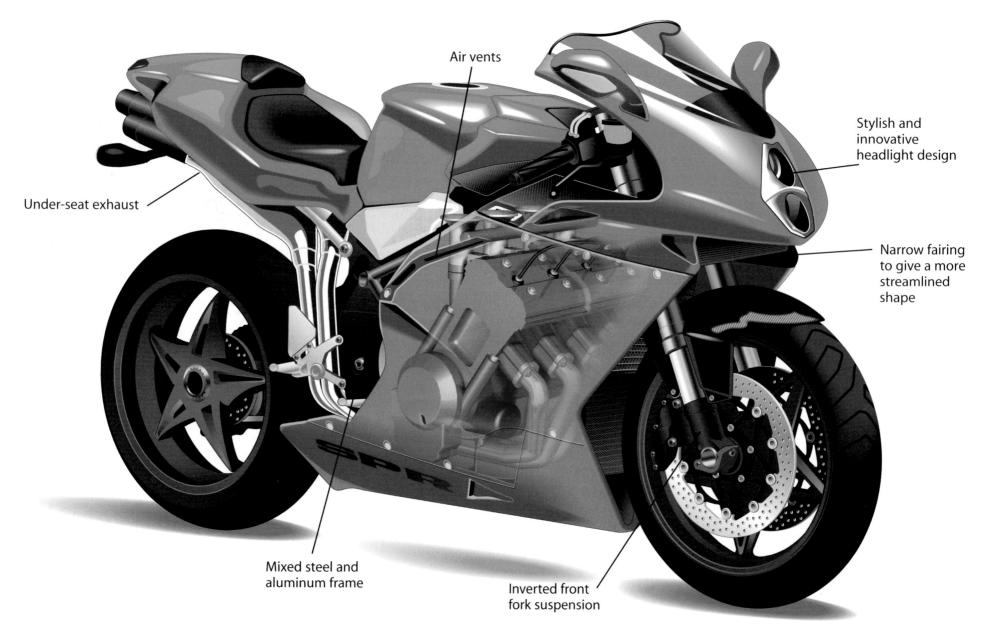

Air vents

Stylish and innovative headlight design

Under-seat exhaust

Narrow fairing to give a more streamlined shape

Mixed steel and aluminum frame

Inverted front fork suspension

Italian manufacturers such as Ferrari and Lamborghini would have to be at the top of a list of makers of the world's most beautiful cars. However, their two-wheel rival is undoubtedly MV Agusta, who have a reputation for producing fast machines. But being Italian means that style matters to them, too. In the 1990s this flair for design created one of the world's most desirable superbikes ever—the F4.

A Design Classic

ABOVE: Agusta's daring idea of putting the exhaust under the seat is the trademark of MV designer Massimo Tamburini. Tamburini also worked on the Ducati 916, which shares the same exhaust layout.

What's in a Name?

Strange as it sounds, until the F4 arrived on the production lines in 1998, no one knew for sure what name would be attached to this spectacular new bike.

MV, which stands for "Meccanica Verghera," was founded in 1945 by an Italian count, Domenico Agusta. However, the Agusta company stopped making motorbikes in the 1970s.

ABOVE: The MV Agusta is beautiful as well as fast. It can reach a top speed of 170 mph.

In fact, in Italy, Agusta is now better known as a helicopter manufacturer. The MV name was bought by Claudio Castiglioni, who began working on a new superbike in the 1990s. His partners were Piero Ferrari, Ducati's designer Massimo Tamburini, and Fiat.

The new bike could easily have been produced under any of these well-established names. Castiglioni decided to take a chance, however, and launched the F4 as an MV Agusta. His gamble paid off and the new bike was hailed as a triumph, setting the standard for all MV Agustas to come.

25

HONDA FIRE BLADE (2000)

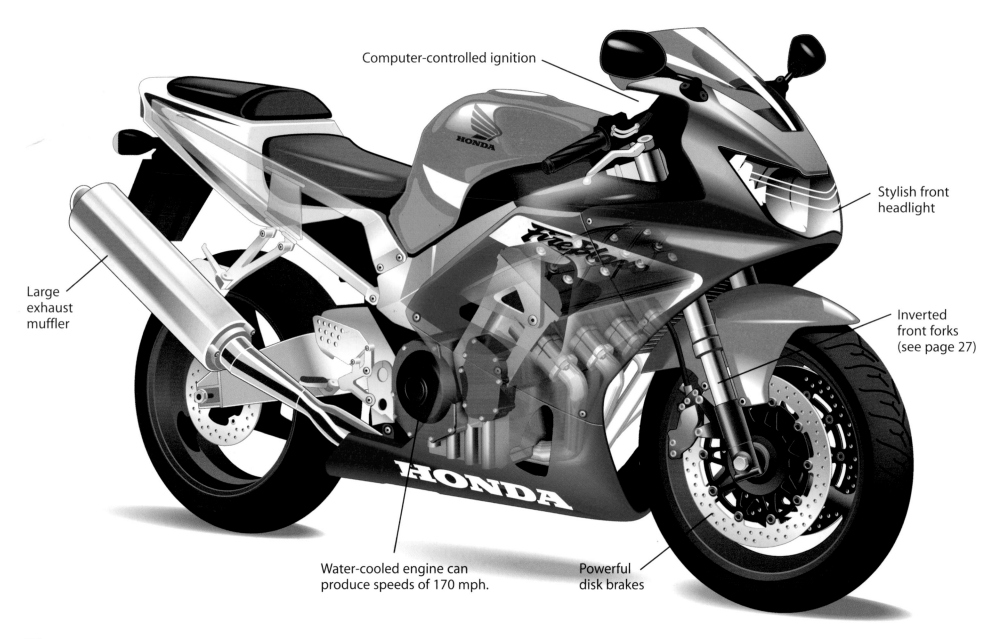

Computer-controlled ignition

Stylish front headlight

Large exhaust muffler

Inverted front forks (see page 27)

Water-cooled engine can produce speeds of 170 mph.

Powerful disk brakes

Honda's CBR900 RR Fire Blade started life in 1992. This groundbreaking motorbike dominated racetracks worldwide, partly due to its combination of lightweight frame and powerful 893 cc (54.5 ci) engine. Honda continued to refine their design over the next eight years. The result was the Fire Blade (2000), which was 32.3 lbs lighter and an average of 10 mph faster than its 1992 big brother.

Telescopic Front Forks

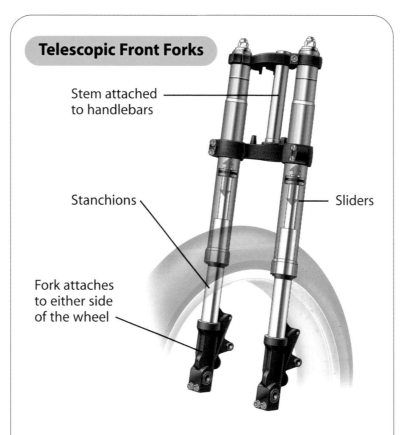

Stem attached to handlebars

Stanchions

Sliders

Fork attaches to either side of the wheel

ABOVE: The bike's wheels are attached to the legs of the fork. On top of these are hollow tubes called "stanchions," which contain springs and dampening mechanisms that work to smooth out the bumps in the road. There are four main types of fork: girder, leading-track, trailing line, and telescopic. This diagram shows an inverted (upside-down) telescopic fork, which is often used on high-performance bikes.

Tire Technology

A tire has two jobs to perform. First, it works with the front fork to give a smoother ride. Second, it makes the bike safer because the treads of the tire, deep grooves in the rubber, help the bike grip the road's surface.

The first "pneumatic" (filled with compressed air) tire was invented by Robert Thomson in 1845 in an attempt to improve riding comfort. If the vehicle was heavy, however, the thin rubber wall of the tire would burst. This problem was solved by lining the inside of the tires. Modern tires are now made up of many layers of rubber, with belts of stretchproof material, like fiberglass, between each layer. This is all woven together with strands of steel wire covered in hardened rubber, producing a hard-wearing tire.

CHAPTER TWO

Racing Cars

People have raced cars in competitions of speed and endurance ever since they were invented, and today motor racing is one of the world's most popular sports.

There's something about a race that excites and delights. The Romans thrilled to the sight of horse-drawn chariots colliding as they raced around specially built arenas. The ancient Chinese celebrated holidays with colorful Dragon Boat races. Eighteenth-century merchants competed to see which sail- or steam-powered ship could cross the oceans the fastest. And when the car was invented, it was only a matter of time before racing models were developed. Today, there are thousands of professional racing events held every year all around the world and, from Formula One to NASCAR, each type of race has its own unique and specially designed cars.

BUGATTI TYPE 35 (1924–1930)

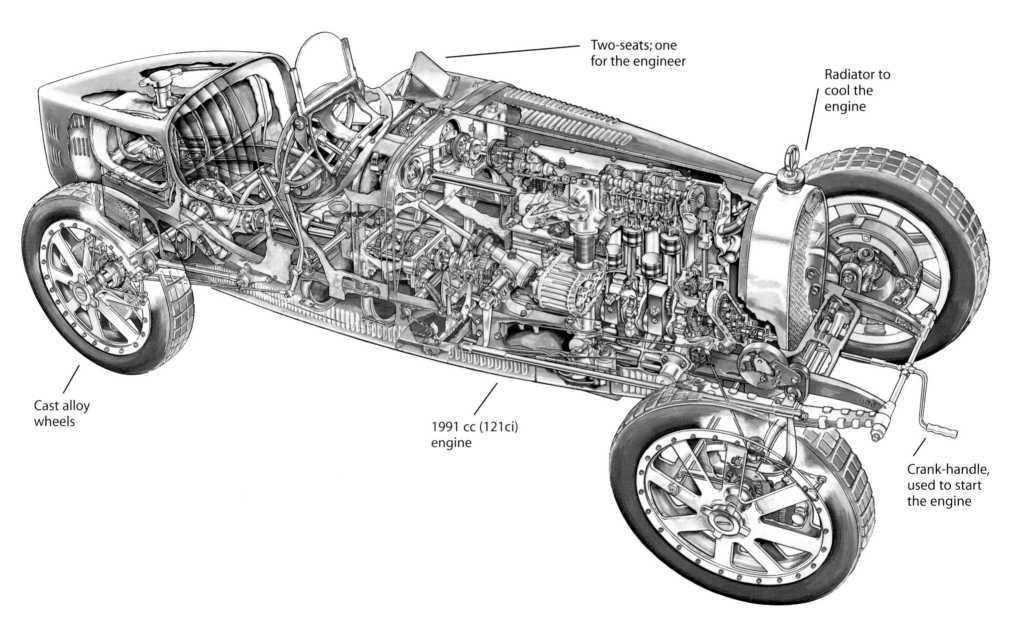

Two-seats; one for the engineer

Radiator to cool the engine

Cast alloy wheels

1991 cc (121ci) engine

Crank-handle, used to start the engine

Ettore Bugatti was trained as an artist, so it's no surprise that each of his carefully crafted machines is a masterpiece in metal. The Type 35, which was launched at the 1924 Lyon Grand Prix, is one of his most beautiful designs. It was also incredibly successful. In total, the Type 35 won more than 1,000 races, including the famous Targa Florio race in Sicily five years running.

Did You Know?

When Ettore Bugatti died in 1947, his family refused to let anyone else design cars under the Bugatti name. This means that every Bugatti that's ever been made was personally designed by the company's founder.

Definitions

Grand Prix: (Meaning "large prize" in French.) A series of races in which cars compete throughout the year for the title of champion.

Vintage Racers

ABOVE: The decade 1922–1933 is known as the "Vintage Period" to race enthusiasts. This is a photograph of the French Grand Prix in 1922.

Vintage Style

The first ever car race, in 1885, was very different from the sort of races that we might see today. Only nine out of the original 22 competitors actually finished— and the average speed was just 15 mph! It was in the 1920s and 1930s that motor racing really began to take off. This was a period when many well-known races were established. The Grand Prix series, for example, began in 1920, and the first Le Mans 24-hour endurance race (see page 37) took place in 1923. It was also a time of great advances in car design. There are three main ways to make a car go faster: Make the engine more powerful; reduce the "drag" (see page 13); or make the car lighter. During this great period of development and experimentation, manufacturers tried all of these techniques, and produced some spectacular cars along the way—so spectacular that today "Vintage Period" racing cars still have a huge fan following.

ABOVE: Refueling was very basic in the early days of racing—this driver is filling his tank with a jug and a funnel!

MERCEDES-BENZ W196 (1954–5)

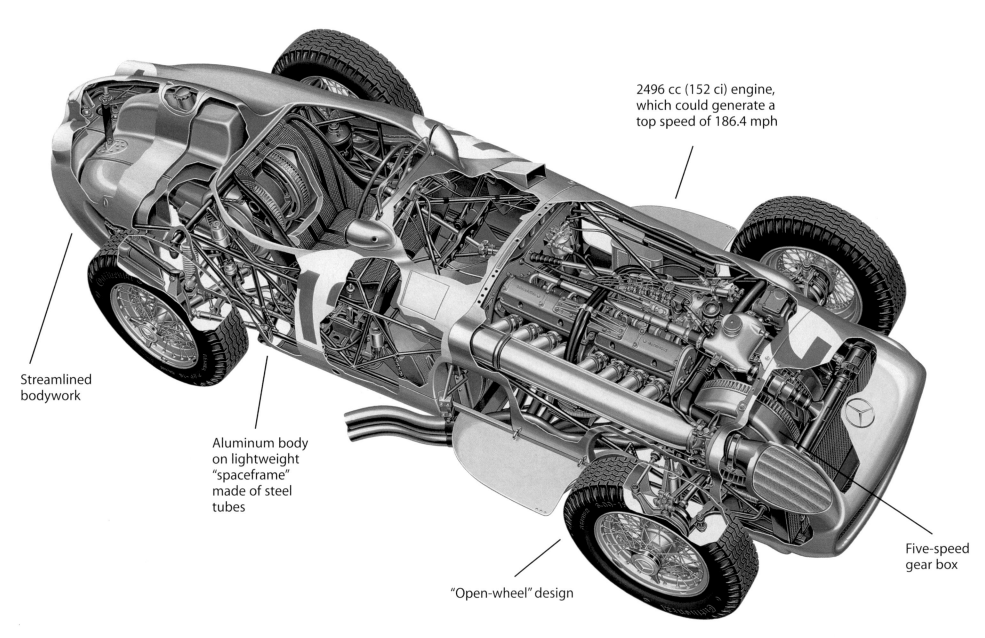

2496 cc (152 ci) engine, which could generate a top speed of 186.4 mph

Streamlined bodywork

Aluminum body on lightweight "spaceframe" made of steel tubes

Five-speed gear box

"Open-wheel" design

Just one look at the Mercedes-Benz W196 will tell you why this sleek racing machine was known as "the Silver Arrow." Like the W25 Silver Arrows produced by Mercedes in the 1930s, both the W196 and the sports model, the W196S "Streamliner," were born race winners. Between 1954 and 1955, the W196 won an incredible nine out of twelve Grands Prix. Designed by Rudulf Uhlenhaut, these were the cars that were responsible for establishing Mercedes-Benz's reputation as a serious competitor to the great Italian designers like Ferrari.

Did You Know?

The original Silver Arrows got their name when Mercedes removed the paintwork to reduce the car's weight!

Stirling Moss and Mercedes: A Great Team

British racing driver Stirling Moss's first big win was at the age of 20, when his privately entered Jaguar XK120 beat Jaguar's own team cars at Britain's most important sports car event, the Tourist Trophy. His big break came in 1955, when he joined Mercedes. Driving the W196S, Moss was simply unbeatable. In that year, he won the Tourist Trophy and the Grand Prix, and set numerous speed records. Sadly, Mercedes pulled out of competitive racing after one of its cars crashed at Le Mans, killing 80 spectators. Moss continued to win titles for other manufacturers, but his time with Mercedes was one of the all-time classic driver-manufacturer combinations.

Definitions
Formula One: Early racing had no restrictions on the size or power of a machine. For fairness, a "formula" of rules was drawn up, which listed the types of cars that could be raced. Over the years, the rules have changed, but the name stuck.

A Winning Team

For more than twenty years, Stirling Moss was the undisputed race car king. Although he never won a World Championship, Moss won 222 of the 495 events that he entered. This incredible record included not only Formula One, but Formulas Two and Three, sports car races, rallies, touring events, and even hill-climbs. Yet, it was when this amazing natural ability was teamed with cutting-edge German engineering that the titles and trophies really started to roll in.

FERRARI 250 GTO (1962–4)

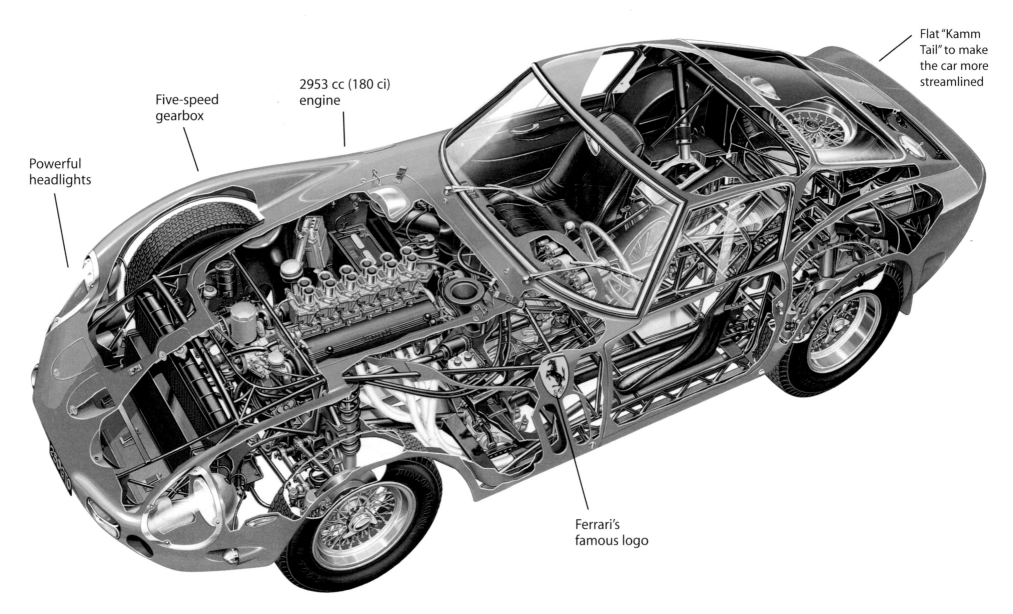

Flat "Kamm Tail" to make the car more streamlined

2953 cc (180 ci) engine

Five-speed gearbox

Powerful headlights

Ferrari's famous logo

It's been said that Ferrari's 250 GTO is the car that set the standard for all future sports cars, both on and off the track. Since its first appearance in 1962, the GTO's low, aluminum body and flat rear "Kamm Tail" design (named after its designer, German engineer Wunibald Kamm) has been imitated by dozens of manufacturers. Yet, while other cars may look similar, none can match Ferrari's 2953 cc (180 ci) engine, which is capable of top speeds in excess of 170 mph.

Did You Know?

Ferrari's well-known prancing horse logo is based on the squadron badge of the famous Italian World War I fighter pilot, Francesco Baracca.

Tuned-up Tourers

ABOVE: A Mercedes-Benz CLK GTR takes a pit stop for fuel during the 1998 FIA (Fédération Internationale de L'Automobile) GT Championship. "Grand Touring" events such as this may take place over several days and cover thousands of miles.

Taking the Tour

Formula One cars are high-performance machines designed with one thing in mind: speed. It is for this reason that Formula One is the racing world's most expensive and dangerous event. However, in Europe and America, more "down-to-earth" cars also race. NASCAR and European "Super Touring" cars are, in fact, ordinary two- or four-door family sedans that have been adapted for the race circuit. "Grand Touring" cars are two-seater coupés that have been "tuned up" for long-distance racing. Touring cars, like the Ferrari, are often labeled "GT" for "Grand Touring," although they also take part in specialist sports car events like Le Mans (see page 37). The "O" in "GTO" stands for "omologato," meaning that the car has been accepted for racing. GTs do not match the speed of Formula One cars, nor cost anywhere near as much, but for millions of fans they are just as thrilling to watch.

FORD GT40 (1967)

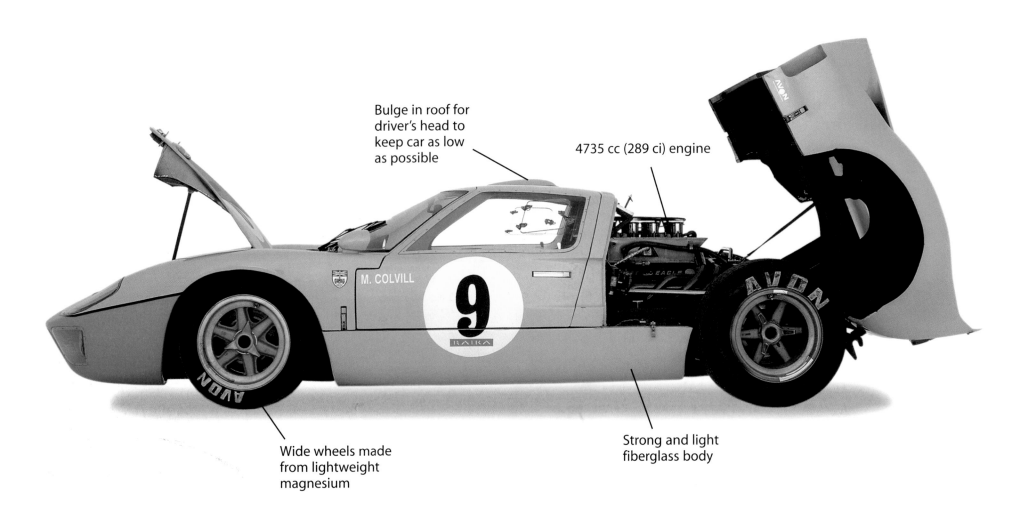

Bulge in roof for driver's head to keep car as low as possible

4735 cc (289 ci) engine

Wide wheels made from lightweight magnesium

Strong and light fiberglass body

Ford's GT40 was built with just one aim: to win the Le Mans 24-hour race. Ferrari had won this world-famous sports car endurance race four years running (from 1958 to 1962), and Ford desperately wanted to prove that an American-made car could not only compete with but also beat the best in the world. Unfortunately Ford's first GT40, the Mark I, failed to even finish the race in 1964. In 1966, however, Ford hit pay dirt and, after that, GT40s won for four consecutive years.

Winning at Le Mans

ABOVE: A Ford GT40 driven by Jackie Ickx and Jackie Oliver wins the 1969 Le Mans 24-hour race just yards ahead of the second-place Porsche.

establish a long-distance endurance race as an annual event, to encourage competition between car manufacturers. This meant that to do well, a car didn't just have to be fast, it also had to perform well over a period of time. The first "24 Heures du Mans" took place on May 26, 1923, and the race continues to attract huge crowds. It's also still an important testing ground for new car designs. In fact, your family sedan car may well include designs that were tried and tested at Le Mans.

ABOVE: The Bentley No. 7 car that won the 2003 Le Mans race—the first victory for Bentley since 1930.

Did You Know?

Between 1903 and 1908, all of Ford's cars were named after letters of the alphabet.

24 Hours to Win!

The Le Mans 24-hour race is one of Europe's most popular and respected sports car races. Racing at Le Mans has a long history: The first ever Grand Prix was held at Le Mans in 1906. That race is now considered to be the ancestor of all Formula One races. In the 1920s, a French automobile club decided to

LOLA T900 (1985)

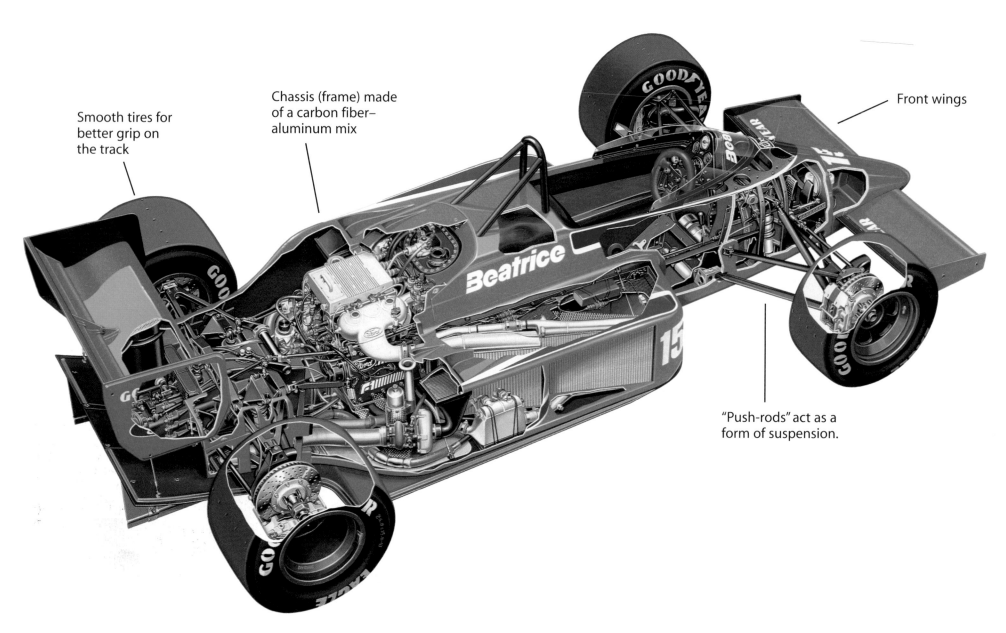

Smooth tires for better grip on the track

Chassis (frame) made of a carbon fiber–aluminum mix

Front wings

"Push-rods" act as a form of suspension.

In the 1960s Lola was one of the world's largest manufacturers of specialized race cars. They built and designed for both Honda and Ford, among others. However, during the 1980s and 1990s their greatest successes came with cars that carried the Lola name. The beautiful T900 was raced by Mario Andretti, who notched up three wins in the world-famous CART Championships.

Did You Know?

Eric Broadly, who founded Lola Cars, was also the consultant engineer on the Ford GT40 (see pages 36–37).

Definitions
CART: (Meaning "Championship Automobile Racing Teams.") This is the U.S. equivalent of European Formula One racing. CART cars are called Champ or IndyCars, after the Indianapolis 500 race.

A Dangerous Profession

If something goes wrong with a regular car traveling at just 50 mph, the driver will be lucky to get out alive. In Formula One and CART racing, cars regularly reach speeds of 200 mph. At these speeds, the slightest engine fault, problem on the track, or lack of concentration on the part of the driver can kill. So racing cars are designed to be tough. The chassis of CART and Formula One cars are made in much the same way as the body of an airplane, and are meant to be just as strong. If the car does break up on impact, the driver is also protected by his clothing. The most important item is the helmet, made from the same light, tough carbon fiber as the chassis. If it's damaged—even scratched—it's replaced. The driver's overalls are made of Nomex, a fire-resistant material. The rules state that it must be able to withstand temperatures of 1290°F for at least 12 seconds—hopefully enough time to be rescued from a burning car!

Spectacular Smashes

ABOVE: Powerful racing car engines often overheat and explode, as this photograph of a Lola T97/00 shows.

MCLAREN MP4/4 (1988)

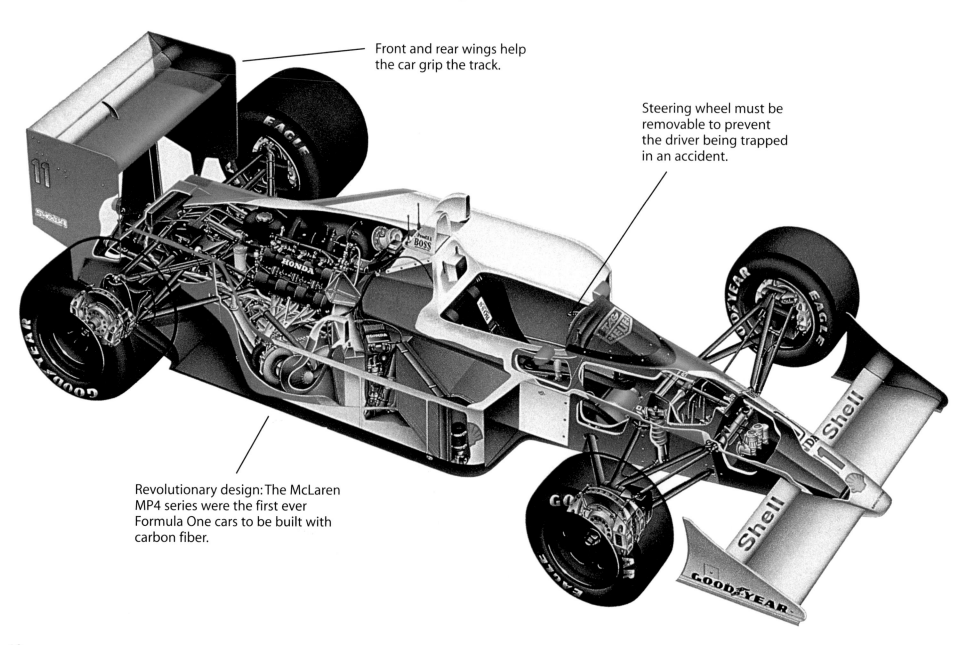

Front and rear wings help the car grip the track.

Steering wheel must be removable to prevent the driver being trapped in an accident.

Revolutionary design: The McLaren MP4 series were the first ever Formula One cars to be built with carbon fiber.

Racing success relies on a combination of great designers and world-class drivers. In 1984, the McLaren team got the mix just right when drivers Alain Prost and Niki Lauda drove their MP4/2s as though they were the only ones in the competition. The result was an incredible first and second placing in the championship. In 1988, the MP4/4 produced another double-whammy. This time, Ayrton Senna took the world title and Prost settled for second.

Did You Know?

In total, the MP4 series won seven Formula One World Championship titles.

A Grand Prix Car's Skeleton Revealed

ABOVE: McLaren driver Alain Prost seated in an MP4/4 in 1988. With the fiberglass bodyshell removed, the carbon fiber tub is clearly visible.

New Materials

The "tub" lies at the heart of a Formula One car. Along with around 70 percent of the car's components, the tub, which includes the driver's cockpit, attached to the engine and front suspension, is made of a tough, lightweight material. This is to protect the driver during crashes. McLaren was one of the first teams to use carbon fiber. Previously, aluminum had been used. It is very light, which is great for a racing car, but it doesn't offer much protection for the driver in the event of an accident. Carbon fiber is four times stiffer than steel and five times stronger. However, it's a difficult substance to work with, as thin layers have to be built up on top of each other, a little like papier mâché. The components also have to be glued together, rather than welded. This makes the process very expensive. A carbon fiber steering wheel, for example, would cost around $120,000!

41

ALFA ROMEO 155 TS (1992–6)

Extra steel framework helps to protect driver.

Powerful headlights

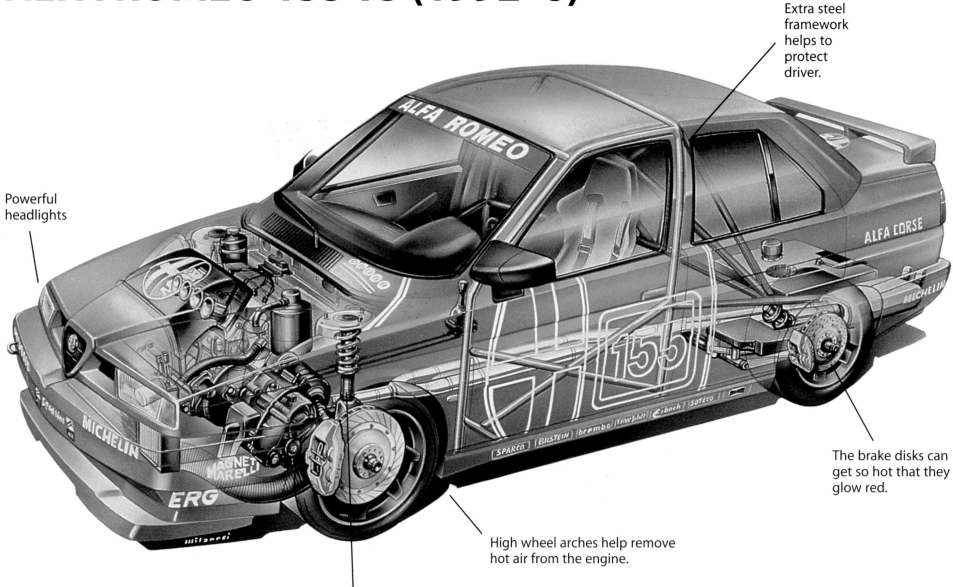

The brake disks can get so hot that they glow red.

High wheel arches help remove hot air from the engine.

Coil springs and "dampers" give all round-suspension.

The Alfa Romeo 155 TS was built to take the stresses and strains inflicted on it by Super Touring events. Like most of the cars that were designed to take part in Europe's version of NASCAR racing, the Alfa Romeo is, on the outside, a sporty-looking four-door sedan. Inside, it's fitted with a powerful engine, six-speed gearbox, and a sturdy suspension—making it every inch the thoroughbred racer.

Did You Know?

The "Alfa" in Alfa Romeo stands for the name of the original company established by Ugo Stella in 1909—"Anonima Lombardo Fabbrica Automobili." The company was bought by Nicola Romeo during World War I.

What an Airbox Does

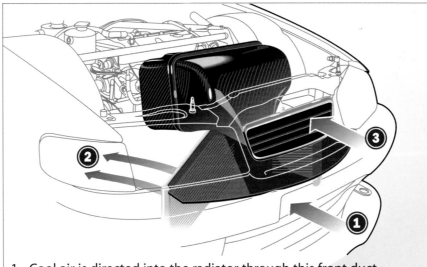

1. Cool air is directed into the radiator through this front duct.
2. Hot air from the radiator is removed from the engine through the wheel arches.
3. Steady supply of cool air enters the air box here.

Racing car engines get very hot, so a complex system keeps things from overheating. A radiator cools down the engine by pumping water around the system. Air from outside is directed into the engine through intake ducts. This stops the water in the radiator from boiling, and also cools down the engine. The airbox's job is to keep the cool air that enters via the radiator grille separate from the hot, directing it to where it's needed most.

Touring Tires

In a high-performance car, every piece of machinery and every accessory is equally important. The right wheels can make a great difference to the speed and handling of a racing car. For Super Touring, light wheels, made from a magnesium alloy, are used to reduce the car's weight. The size of the tires is also an important consideration. Racing tires are wider and larger than ordinary tires. This helps the tire grip the road and gives the driver more control at high speeds.

PENSKE PC18 (1989)

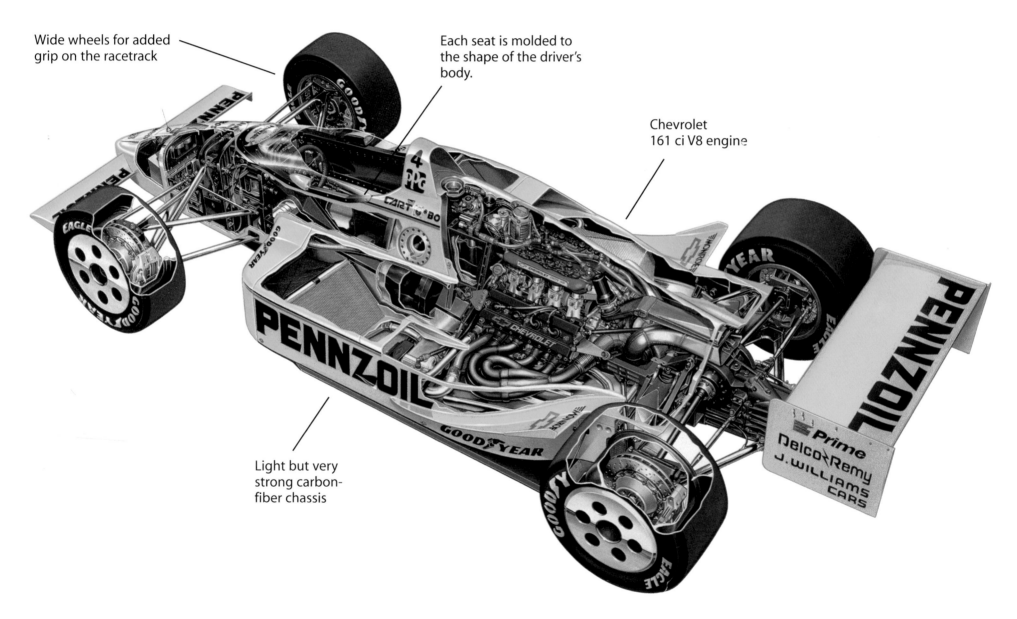

Wide wheels for added
grip on the racetrack

Each seat is molded to
the shape of the driver's
body.

Chevrolet
161 ci V8 engine

Light but very
strong carbon-
fiber chassis

Team Penske is the most successful IndyCar team ever. Since Penske Racing was founded in 1966, boss Roger Penske and his team of dedicated drivers and engineers have worked their way into the history books. In less than 40 years, Penske has notched up over 100 Indy race wins. This includes a dozen victories at the Indianapolis 500, which is one of the toughest events of the racing year. And they did it all with cars like the PC18.

Did You Know?

Before Team Penske was formed, Roger Penske was a successful driver in his own right and was named *New York Times* "Driver of the Year" in 1962.

Looking Back . . .

Technology has come a long way since this 1954 Kuzma roadster was driven in the Indianapolis 500. Compared to modern racing cars like the PC18, this looks more like a tractor! Apart from its shape, the most obvious difference is that, in a modern Indy racer, the engine is toward the back of the car. Manufacturers had experimented with front and mid-engined machines since the 1930s, but it was a Cooper Climax T53 that proved they could be race winners. First driven by Stirling Moss (see page 33) at the Argentine Grand Prix in 1957, the T53 started the rear-engine revolution.

Show Me the Money!

In the days of Vintage racing, almost anyone could get in on the act. All you needed was mechanical skill and time, as many cars were "home-builds"! In today's Formula One and CART racing, independent drivers (those not under contract to a team) are rare: Racing is expensive. McLaren spends around $500 million a year, so it needs sponsors to pay the bills. And that's why you will see company logos on billboards, on the side of cars, and even on the driver's overalls.

FERRARI F3000 (1998)

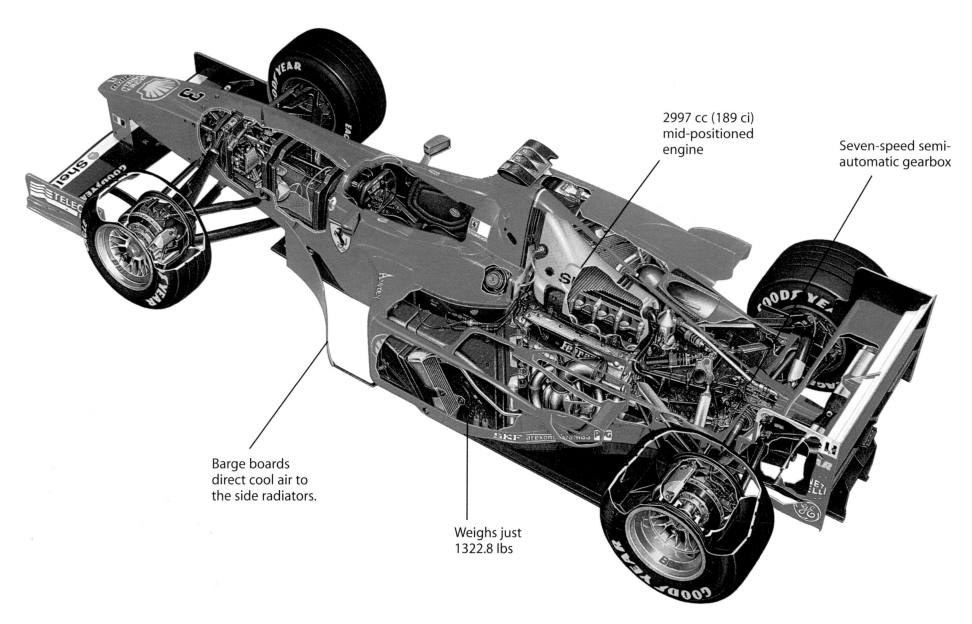

2997 cc (189 ci) mid-positioned engine

Seven-speed semi-automatic gearbox

Barge boards direct cool air to the side radiators.

Weighs just 1322.8 lbs

With its rich, racing-red livery and consistently good racetrack performances, Ferrari has been a racegoer's favorite since Enzo Ferrari built his first classic car. For drivers and their teams, though, the ultimate accomplishment is to have their hard work recognized by people in the same business. This is exactly what happened to the Ferrari F3000. Thanks to an entirely new engine and chassis design, this stunning racing machine was awarded the Constructor's Prize in 1999 in recognition of the ground-breaking work of its engineering and design team.

Definitions

livery: The distinctive uniform or badge of a company.

Smooth Lines

ABOVE: The rear of the Ferrari F3000 is designed in a "coke bottle" shape to help the air to flow as smoothly as possible over the car.

What Are Aerodynamics?

We know that the shape of an object is important. A streamlined shape will reduce the amount of drag created by the air or water passing over a moving object (see page 13). Aerodynamics is a science that helps us to decide what types of streamlined shapes might work best in different circumstances. For example, when the Wright Brothers were designing their airplane, they used aerodynamics to work out what shape the wings needed to be to help keep the plane in the air. Aerodynamics are important in almost all forms of transport, apart from spacecraft—once these are in space, there's no air to create drag. In racing cars, a good streamlined shape is one that reduces drag but also helps to keep the car stable. When you're traveling at very high speeds, the force of the wind will buffet the car around, and can force it off the road. Formula One and CART cars get around this by being very close to the road's surface. This brings another aerodynamic principle, called downforce, into play. Downforce is explained on page 49.

Did You Know?

Since their first race in 1947, Ferraris have had over 5,000 successful races on tracks all over the world.

LOTUS ELISE SPORT (2000)

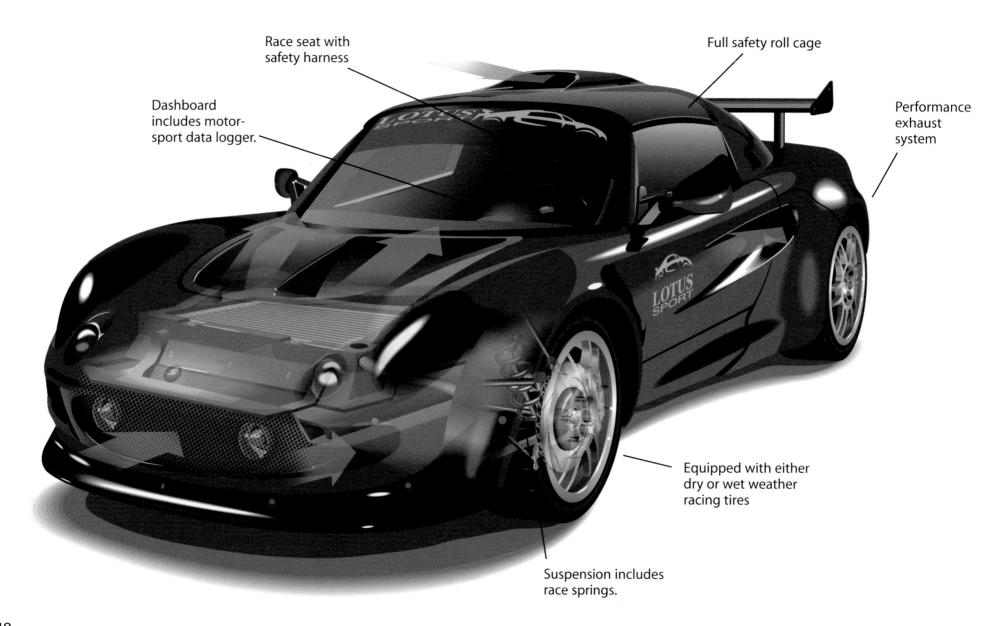

Race seat with safety harness

Dashboard includes motor-sport data logger.

Full safety roll cage

Performance exhaust system

Equipped with either dry or wet weather racing tires

Suspension includes race springs.

The most surprising thing about the Lotus Elise Sport is that it is powered by exactly the same Rover 1,796 cc (110 ci) engine as the popular roadgoing model. However, this stunning sports car is much more than an ordinary family coupé. Capable of accelerating from 0–60 mph in just 5.4 seconds, this is one of the world's fastest sports cars.

Why Racing Cars Have Wings

How Downforce Works

Downforce varies with a car's speed. For a car with an aerodynamic shape, more downforce will be created as the car speeds up. The maximum downforce for a Formula One car occurs at between 93 and 124 mph. At this speed, the air pressure pushing down on the car equals its weight. In theory, the car could drive upside down on the roof of a tunnel without falling off! At top speeds, downforce exerts a pressure that is twice the weight of the car. On corners, this means that drivers experience high g-forces, just like fighter pilots.

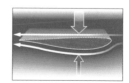

Airplane wings are flat on the bottom and curved on the top. When a plane is stationary, the air pressure under it is the same as above it. Once its wing is moving through the air, this changes. The curved surface on the top of the wing slows down the air as it passes over it. Under the wing, the air is traveling over a flat surface, so it stays the same. This creates a difference in air pressure, which helps to lift the plane up. In a racing car, drivers must keep the car down on the ground, so wings are added, like an upside-down version of those on a plane. So, instead of lifting, they push the car down. This is called downforce.

Did You Know?

Ten percent of all new cars made in Europe have Lotus-developed engines.

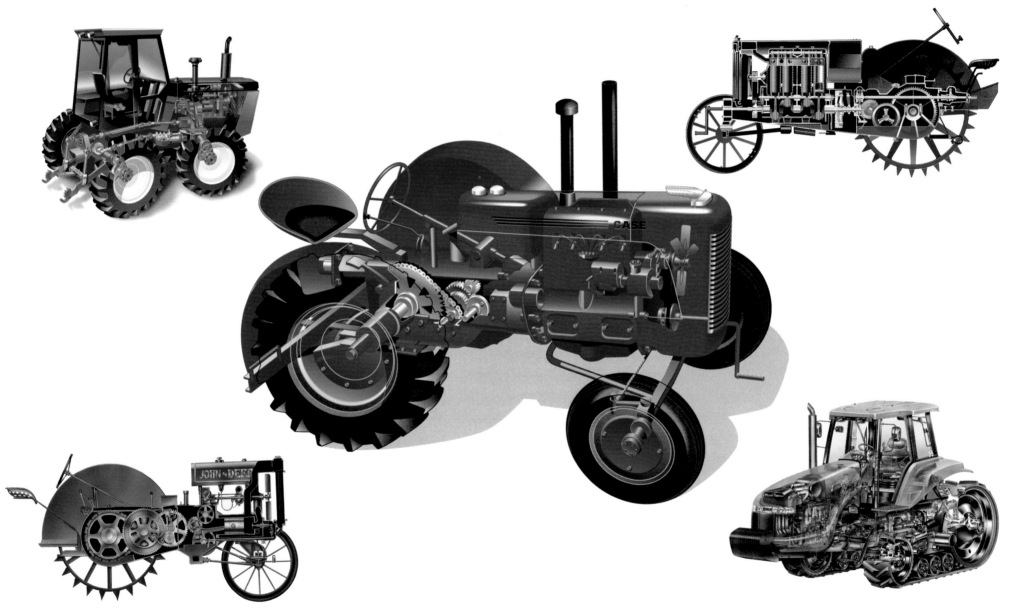

CHAPTER THREE

Tractors

Designed to take over the hard work once carried out by farmers and their animals, these mechanical marvels have changed the face of the countryside.

In the eighteenth century, life on the farm was tough. In the spring, soil had to be tilled and seeds planted. In the summer, there were crops to be gathered, vegetables to be dug, and wheat to cut and thresh. Work days were long and farmers and their animals often worked from sunup to sunset. The arrival of the tractor changed all of that. It's true that the early machines were big and cumbersome, but they could do the work of a dozen people and pull a plow or harvester harder than any horse. Within just one generation, the only horsepower that most farmers were interested in was the one created by a combustion engine.

JOHN DEERE D (1923)

Simple metal
seat

Basic kerosene/paraffin engine

Deere's famous "leaping deer"
logo and green paintwork

Gears—two
forward and one
reverse

The secret to John Deere's success was simplicity. While most tractor manufacturers in the 1920s were developing faster, more powerful four-cylinder engines for their machines, the Model D used a two-cylinder design. These were big, slow engines. They were also simple to use, easy to repair, cheap, and dependable, which made them incredibly popular. Between 1923 and 1929, John Deere sold 10,000 Model Ds, and the design was so successful that it continued to be the farmer's tractor of choice until production stopped in 1953.

Did You Know?

The Model D's two-cylinder engine made a distinctive "popping" noise, which earned it the nickname "Poppin' Johnny."

Past Glories

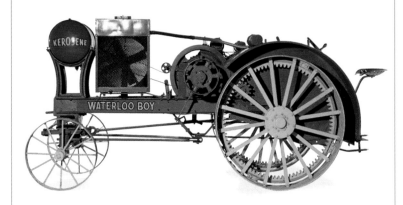

Think of tractors, and it's hard not to think of John Deere. Over 160 years, the company, which was founded by a blacksmith from Vermont, has become one of the most recognized names in the industry. Yet it wasn't until 1918 that John Deere went into the tractor business. The turning point came when the president of the Waterloo Gasoline Traction Engine Company decided to retire. John Deere was a company already respected for its range of farm equipment, and it made no secret of being interested in starting tractor production. All it needed was a factory. By buying the Traction Engine Company for $2,100,000, it got much more. The Waterloo Boy was the first tractor sold by John Deere and its distinctive engine formed the basis for Deere's own Model D.

A Design in Demand

The Model D's two-cylinder engine made it very fuel-efficient, and therefore cheap to run. At the heart of this successful design was the Schebler fuel primer and carburetor, shown. This is the part of the engine that controls the supply of air and fuel to the cylinders. Today, early John Deeres are sought after by tractor collectors who admire the simplicity and practicality of the design. As many of the Model Ds were used for decades, farmers often made their own modifications to the engines. This makes models with original engines especially desirable.

FORDSON MODEL N (1929)

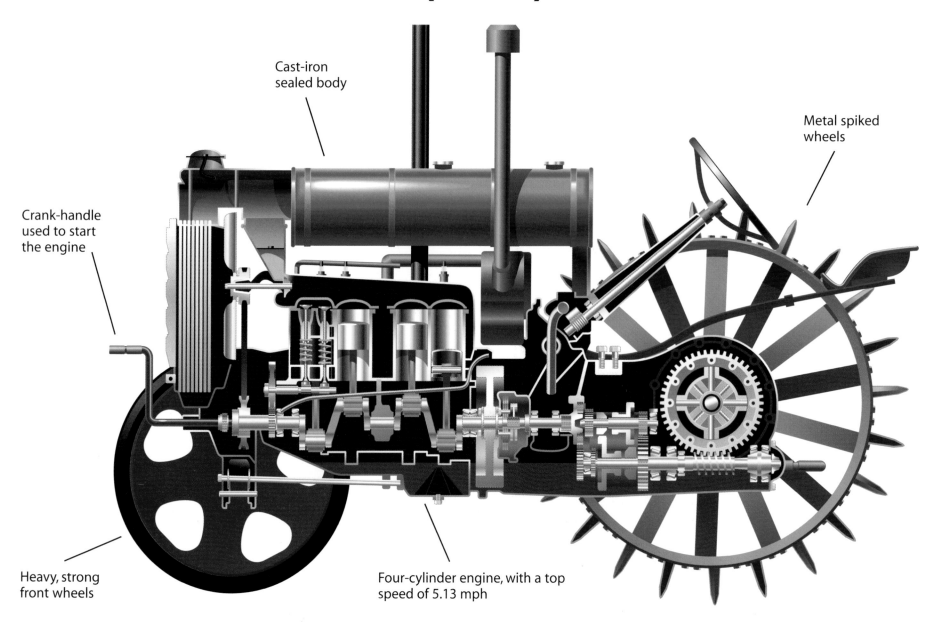

Cast-iron
sealed body

Metal spiked
wheels

Crank-handle
used to start
the engine

Heavy, strong
front wheels

Four-cylinder engine, with a top
speed of 5.13 mph

Henry Ford had made cheap, mass-produced cars available to everyone, and he believed that by using the same production-line methods he could make farm machines that were just as affordable. As a farmer's son, he was aware just how hard the work on a farm could be and he wanted to produce huge numbers of low-priced, well-designed tractors. The result was the Model N. These early metal marvels revolutionized farm work and removed much of the backbreaking manual labor that farmers had previously accepted as a fact of life.

Did You Know?

In the early 1920s, 70 percent of all tractors sold in America were Fordsons.

Henry Ford (1863–1947)

ABOVE: Henry Ford pictured on one of his own models.

Affordable Fordson

The first Fordson tractor was manufactured in 1917, during World War I. At the request of the British government, which desperately needed farm machinery to replace the men and horses sent to the trenches, the design of the Model F was completed in record time. Despite this, it was one of the most successful tractors ever built. Light, powerful, and relatively small, compared to its competitors, the F set the standard for all future tractors. In time, other models appeared, and all had one thing in common—a reasonable price. In 1917, a Model F cost $750, and by 1922, just $395. The Model N was even cheaper. Ford believed that by increasing food production, he could improve life for ordinary people, so he kept the price of his tractors low to make them available to as many farmers as possible. He was especially generous to the new Soviet state. Within a few years, 85 percent of all tractors in Russia were Fordsons, and most were probably sold at a loss!

ALLIS-CHALMERS U (1929)

Powerful engine could reach speeds of 35 mph.

Large padded seat for the driver

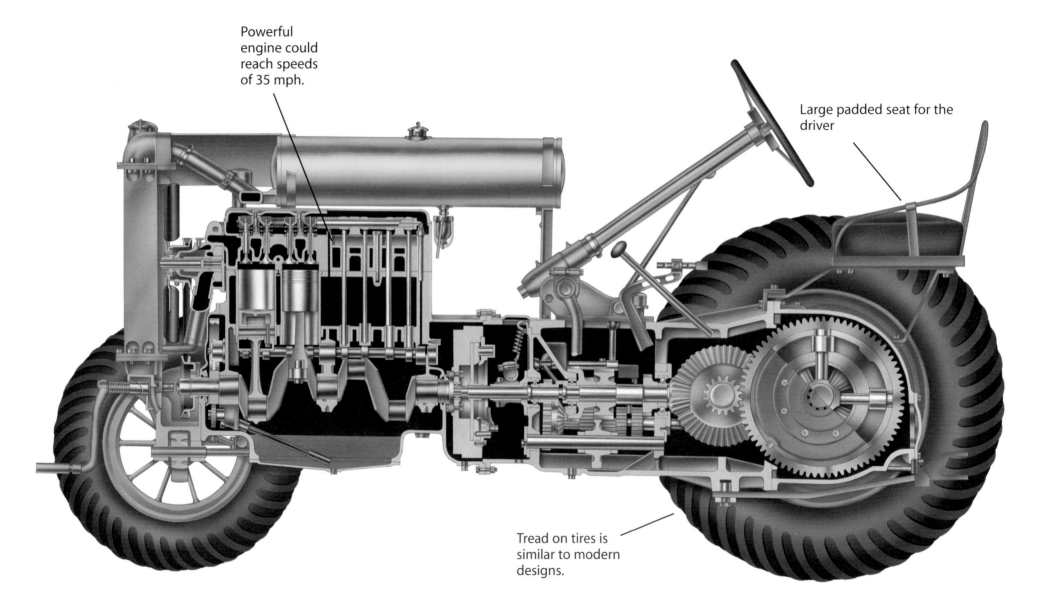

Tread on tires is similar to modern designs.

One look at the Allis-Chalmers U tells you why this tractor made it into the history books. This powerful machine was the first to use inflatable rubber tires. Today, big, chunky tires are used on most tractors and trucks, but when these were introduced in 1929 farmers couldn't believe that they would work in muddy fields and on rough track roads. Allis-Chalmers proved their point by hiring racing drivers to show how well these new tires performed. Farmers, and Allis's rivals, were so impressed that within a few years half of all tractors sold used pneumatic tires.

Did You Know?

The tires used on the Model U were similar to those used on aircraft.

Big and Beautiful

ABOVE: Large inflatable rubber tires are now a familiar sight on farm and construction-site vehicles.

Under Pressure

Tractors were designed to pull agricultural machinery, like plows, but farmers soon realized that they could be useful for all sorts of other jobs around the farm too. The problem was that until the Model U, most tractors had hard, studded metal wheels, which were designed to grip in soil, but which would tear up road surfaces. Pneumatic tires could be filled with air under pressure, which made them hard enough to cope with uneven surfaces, yet soft enough to be acceptable on public roads. By fitting pneumatic tires, the Allis-Chalmers Model U was turned from a piece of farm machinery into a multipurpose vehicle. Not only that, but tests proved that pneumatic tires saved fuel. The fact that they were easier to handle and could be driven on roads rather than just dirt tracks made them much more efficient. A standard Model U might cost around $200 more than other tractors but, in just over a month, the farmer could save that much on gas. In fact, over a year, a tractor with rubber tires would actually save the farmer around $1400!

Definitions
pneumatic: Filled with air under pressure.

MASSEY-HARRIS 25 (1931)

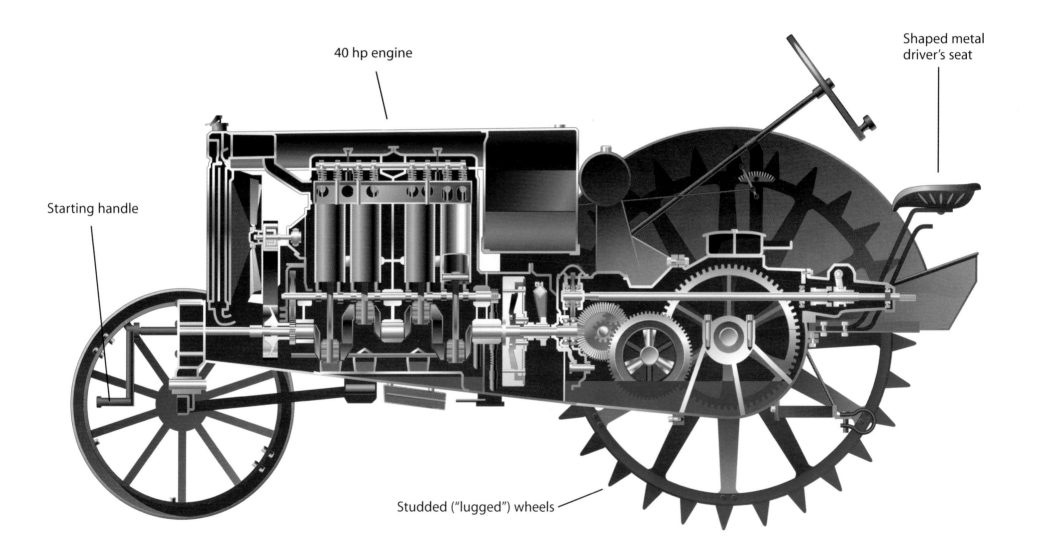

40 hp engine

Shaped metal
driver's seat

Starting handle

Studded ("lugged") wheels

In technical terms, the Massey-Harris Model 25 was a bit of a jumble. It was based on Wallis's U-Frame 20-30 Tractor, which Massey had inherited when it took over the J.I. Case Plough Works in 1929. With an upgraded engine and gearbox, the Model 25 wasn't a revolutionary tractor, but it did give Massey-Harris just what it needed to establish itself in the booming tractor business: a tough, reliable workhorse that didn't cost a fortune to make.

Did You Know?

In the 1920s, the average tractor engine produced around 20–30 hp. For its time, the Model 25 was incredibly powerful. Modern tractor engines can produce 100–300 hp.

A New Design for Stronger Tractors

ABOVE: The key to a successful tractor was a strong but accessible frame. This photo shows a Wallis Cub, which introduced the patented U Frame design in 1913. The steel U-Frame supported the engine and gearbox.

Definitions

hp: (Meaning horsepower.) A measurement of the amount of work, in terms of power, that an engine can do. One horsepower is equal to 745.7 watts.

What Was the U-Frame?

Early tractors like the Waterloo Boy (see page 53) had an "open frame" design. The frame, which held the engine and gears, was usually made of steel girders to be as strong as possible. An open frame made it easy to repair the tractor, but also left delicate engine parts exposed to the elements. When Ford's designers were developing his Model F, they ditched the frame entirely. Their "frameless" design joined the engine and gears together in one sealed cast-iron case. This protected the engine parts but made it difficult for farmers to make repairs. The Wallis Company came up with another solution: They developed their own U-Frame, which protected the underside of the engine and gave additional structural strength. When Massey-Harris bought Wallis, the $2.9 million deal included the patent to the U Frame, which featured in all Massey-Harris tractors until the 1940s.

59

CASE LA (1940)

Lever-operated clutch enables driver to select from four forward gears and one reverse.

More curved appearance than the Model L

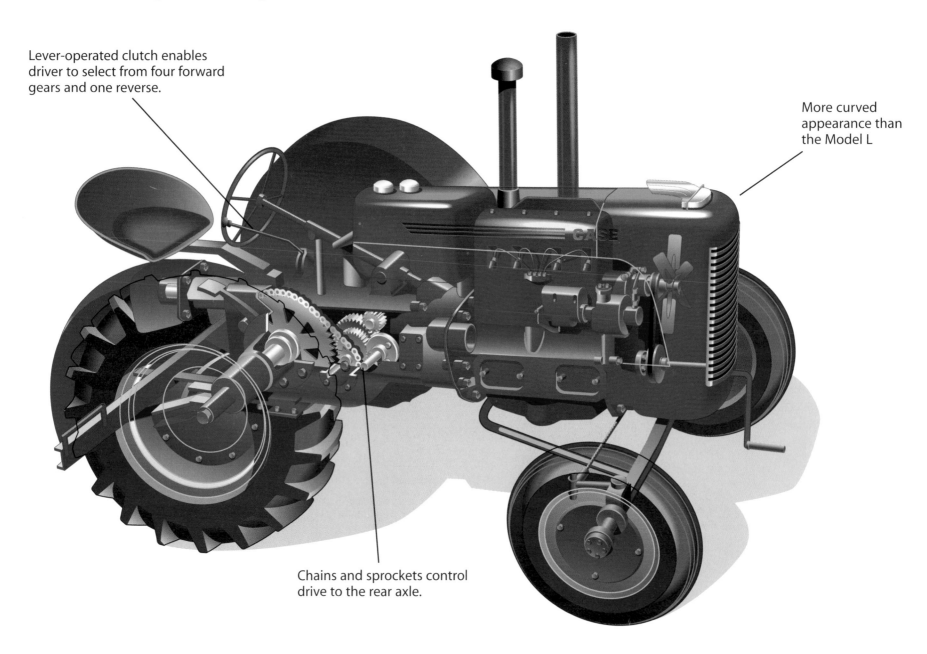

Chains and sprockets control drive to the rear axle.

The J.I. Case Company is one of the most famous names in American farming history. With its distinctive bright orange paintwork and bald eagle logo, Case was one of the original pioneers of tractor manufacture. The Model LA, which was a redesigned version of the extremely popular Model L, is an example of the type of sturdy yet stylish and compact designs that made Case a household name.

Big and Heavy Pioneers

ABOVE: Although early tractors like this Rumely oil-powered model were heavy and slow, they were more efficient than doing the job by hand!

stalks. These machines could thresh 300 bushels of wheat a day. Working by hand, a farmer could manage only six! By the 1870s, Case had started to produce steam engines. The first models were pulled by horses, but within ten years, Case had developed a self-propelled model. The company's first gas-powered tractors arrived in 1911. Despite fierce competition from Ford, business boomed. In fact, the company he built is still around today: The Case Corporation makes profits of around $6 billion a year.

Did You Know?

The logo of the J.I. Case Company features a bald eagle called "Old Abe," which belonged to the Eighth Wisconsin Regiment during the American Civil War.

Out With the Old, In With the New

When Jerome Increase Case was a boy, farming relied on manual labor. The farmer would cut the crops by hand, using a curved blade called a scythe. Innovators like Case changed all that. Case was known as the "Threshing Machine King" because his company started out making threshing machines, which were designed to separate the heads of wheat (or similar crops) from their

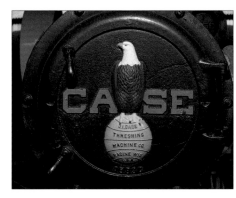

ABOVE: The logo of the J.I. Case Threshing Machine Company.

61

VALMET 705 (1984)

Driver's seat swivels around to enable him to operate both sets of controls.

83 hp, 4.4 liter (269 ci) engine

Two sets of steering controls for forward- or backward-facing operator

Eight forward and four reverse gears

Farm tractors remained almost unchanged in their basic design for much of the first half of the twentieth century. Economic depression and two world wars meant that farmers in the 1930s and '40s simply didn't have the money to spend on big, expensive machines. By the 1960s, however, things were starting to change. A more stable world economy meant more money for investment. For farmers, this brought a range of new developments. One of the most exciting were "bidirectional" (or two-way) tractors such as the Valmet 705.

Comfort Versus Cost

Early tractors were designed to be cheap, not comfortable. Although no farmer really wanted to spend all day perched on a cold, hard, metal seat in the rain, they didn't have the money to spend on what were seen as "luxuries" either. In fact, when Minneapolis-Moline produced the "Comfortractor" in the 1930s, it sold only 150. The Comfortractor came with a fully enclosed cab, a heater, radio, padded seats, a light-up instrument panel, a cigar lighter, and an ash tray. Yet it cost twice as much as a standard tractor with a metal seat, so nobody wanted to buy one. The big breakthrough came in the 1960s, when a survey looked at how well tractors actually performed compared to the maker's claims. Most underperformed, but not because the makers had lied. It was just that the tractors were too

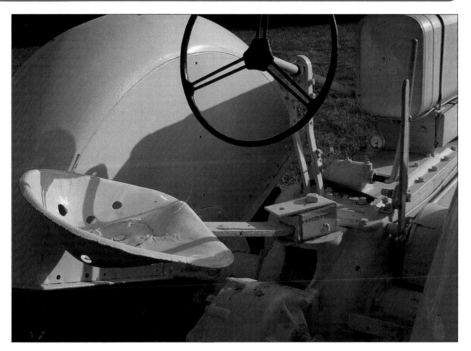

ABOVE: For well over half a century, most tractors have only had a shaped metal seat mounted on a springy steel support. Ouch!

uncomfortable to be used at top speeds for long periods of time. A better suspension and comfortable cab weren't luxuries. If farmers wanted to get the best from their expensive machinery, they were a necessity! Tractors like the Valmet OY 705 were the first of a new generation to combine power and performance with comfort.

VERSATILE 256 BIDIRECTIONAL (1984)

The driver's seat and steering wheel are joined, and can swivel 180 degrees if the tractor is working in reverse.

100 hp, 3.9 liter (239 cu in) engine

Deeply ridged tires

Hydraulic drawbar

In 1957, two Minnesota brothers decided that they needed a more powerful tractor to handle the work on their 4,000-acre farm. The result was a tractor that boasted a 130 hp engine and four-wheel drive. This "home-build" was so successful that they soon had to set up a workshop to cope with requests for similar machines from their neighbors. Today the Versatile factory provides a range of big, powerful, and innovative tractors such as the 256.

Definitions
four-wheel drive: Where the engine's power is distributed evenly through all four wheels. This gives the driver more maneuverability and control. See also page 101.

Bigger Isn't Always Better

Specialized machines are expensive, so over the years designers have looked at ways of making tractors even more flexible. This massive eight-wheeled machine, called Big Roy, was Versatile's attempt to produce a tractor that would be powerful enough to take on the workload of a large farm while retaining its natural "tractor" flexibility. Unfortunately, it was too specialized and was never developed.

Your Flexible Friend

Tractors were designed to be flexible enough to perform as many different jobs as possible around the farm. By attaching a plow, loader, trailer, mower, bailer, or seed drill to the back of a tractor, a simple engine on wheels can be converted into a piece of specialized equipment. Of course, there are some jobs that tractors can't do well. For specialty crops like cotton, a cotton baler will be more efficient than a tractor adapted for the work. Similarly, on a farm with thousands of acres of wheat, one tractor isn't going to be powerful enough to cut and thresh the crops. A combine harvester is needed. Generally, though, it's the tractor's versatility that has made it a must-have machine.

Did You Know?

Versatile is the world's leading producer of bidirectional tractors.

CATERPILLAR CHALLENGER 55 (1987)

Large driver's cab

Large wheels transmit power to the tracks.

Powerful headlights

Rubber tracks, reinforced with steel cables

Take a look at the Caterpillar Challenger, and one thing is immediately obvious. Like a tank, it has tracks rather than the huge inflated tires that are such a familiar sight on farm machinery. Caterpillar didn't invent "crawlers," but Caterpillar's founders, Benjamin Holt and Daniel Best, were both pioneers—and the company continues to be at the cutting-edge of track technology. The Challenger series, shown here, was the first tractor ever to use rubber tracks.

Did You Know?

Caterpillar changed the color of their paintwork to "Highway Yellow" in 1931 because they felt that people needed cheering up after the economic depression of the 1920s! This is now the standard color of all construction vehicles.

Crawler Kings

BELOW: The Challenger's rubber track, which is called Mobil-trac, was a huge leap forward in crawler design. Rubber tracks are lighter, cheaper, and more reliable than metal tracks.

How Tracks Work

Tracks grip the ground better than wheels because they have a larger surface area in contact with it. This means that a vehicle equipped with tracks is less likely to slip (it has more "traction"), so it can do more work, with less power, using less fuel. Tracks also spread the weight of the machine more evenly, so heavy vehicles on tracks are less likely to sink into mud. It seems surprising, then, that tractors with tracks were a late development. Benjamin Holt and Daniel Best had experimented with tracks as early as 1904, but the track itself presented a problem. Tracks are metal segments connected to form a continuous band, which is driven around by wheels. If one of the segments breaks, or if the track comes off the wheels, it can take a long time to repair. Without the advances in tank track design made during World War I, tracks would have remained too unreliable to use.

CLAAS XERION 2500 (2000)

Bidirectional: up to 31 mph in either direction

Front and rear coupling options

All-wheel drive makes the tractor more maneuverable.

Wheels available in sizes up to 42 inches

Modern farmers demand more from a tractor than just a simple metal seat, a kerosene-powered engine, and a set of solid metal wheels. In the twenty-first century, a tractor must be designed for comfort, safety, efficiency, and high performance. With all-wheel drive, a fuel-saving engine, and a modern high-tech cab, the Xerion series from German manufacturer Claas represents the climax of a century of tractor evolution.

Transformer Tractor

LEFT: The Xerion is the ultimate in modern tractor design. The driver's cab can be completely removed and repositioned, at either the front or back of the tractor, to give additional space to carry heavy loads.

The Shape of Things to Come

What will the farmers of the future want from their tractors? This is the question which modern manufacturers are desperately trying to answer, and the company that guesses right stands to make big money. Over the last century, we've seen the development of bigger, more powerful machines, safer, more comfortable cabs, and a greater versatility of design. As oil reserves run out and public concerns increase about levels of pollution, there are demands for vehicles to be more fuel-efficient. Tractors powered by alternative energy such as oilseed rape already exist, so perhaps the tractor of the future will be one that runs on free, clean energy such as solar power? There's also a move toward more and more tractor systems being computer-controlled. Renault has already demonstrated a remote-controlled tractor that used Global Positioning Satellite (GPS) technology to guide an unmanned cab around a field. Potentially, this means that farmers may soon be able to sow and harvest their crops without ever setting foot in a field! These are just a few of the options available. We'll have to wait and see, but if the last 100 years are anything to go by, any new developments will be good news for the farmers!

ABOVE: This Ares tractor was fitted with an automatic guidance system, which was designed to make the driver's job less stressful.

CHAPTER FOUR

Trucks

*From small-goods vehicles to long-distance haulers, trucks
are essential machines, transporting and delivering
almost everything we use, from food to flowers.*

No one can really claim to have invented the truck. Unlike the motorbike or car, there was no one person whose work came first and made the truck possible. In fact, like all good ideas, necessity was really the mother of this invention. It's hard, in fact, to define exactly what a truck is. We can say that a truck is anything designed to carry a large load, but to truck enthusiasts all over the world, they are more than just mechanical workhorses. The sight of these huge, noisy machines roaring down the highway is an incredible experience. It's no wonder that truckers are sometimes called "kings of the road"!

VOLVO FL SERIES

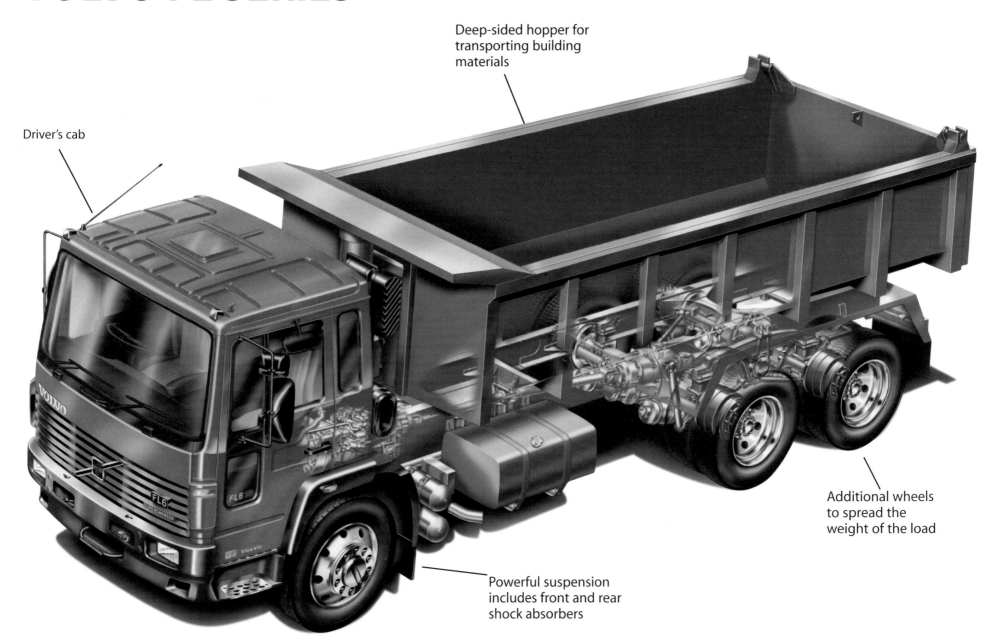

Deep-sided hopper for transporting building materials

Driver's cab

Additional wheels to spread the weight of the load

Powerful suspension includes front and rear shock absorbers

VOLVO

FL6

The FL series is one of Volvo's smallest but most flexible truck ranges. Designed for local and regional deliveries, garbage collection, fire and rescue services, and construction work, the FL series includes the FL12 curtainsider model and the FL626 builder's truck, shown here. Introduced to the United States in 1986, this tough truck is designed to cope with hard, everyday work in the building trade.

Did You Know?

Volvo is Latin for "I roll." The name was chosen because the company's founders, Assar Gabrielsson and Gustaf Larsen, used to work for a Swedish ball-bearing manufacturer.

Definitions

curtainsider: The name given to tall trucks that have open sides covered by flexible plastic "curtains" (drapes).

Bigger Volvo Trucks

ABOVE: The FH range (see pages 86–87) is one of Volvo's most successful ranges of trucks to date. This FH12 features a full-side-opening trailer.

Swedish Style

All good ideas are simple, and it was simplicity that was the key to Volvo's early success. Volvo's first trucks, the Model 1 and Model 2, appeared in 1928 and were basic designs, made with the same components as cars. They lacked pulling power, and could only carry small loads, but they proved to be popular. By the 1930s, the LV series had appeared. This included the LV290, which was nicknamed "long nose" because its hood stuck out

ABOVE: Volvo trucks at work on a construction site in the 1960s.

over its front wheels. This was their largest truck and put them into competition with another firm, Scania-Vabis. However, war in Europe meant that both companies switched to the production of armored military vehicles until the 1940s. Volvo's wartime success allowed the company to expand, and by the 1960s, it boasted a range of trucks as well as a booming car business. Today, Volvo is one of the world's largest manufacturers of heavy vehicles—a true success story.

FREIGHTLINER FLD120, CLASS 8 (1995)

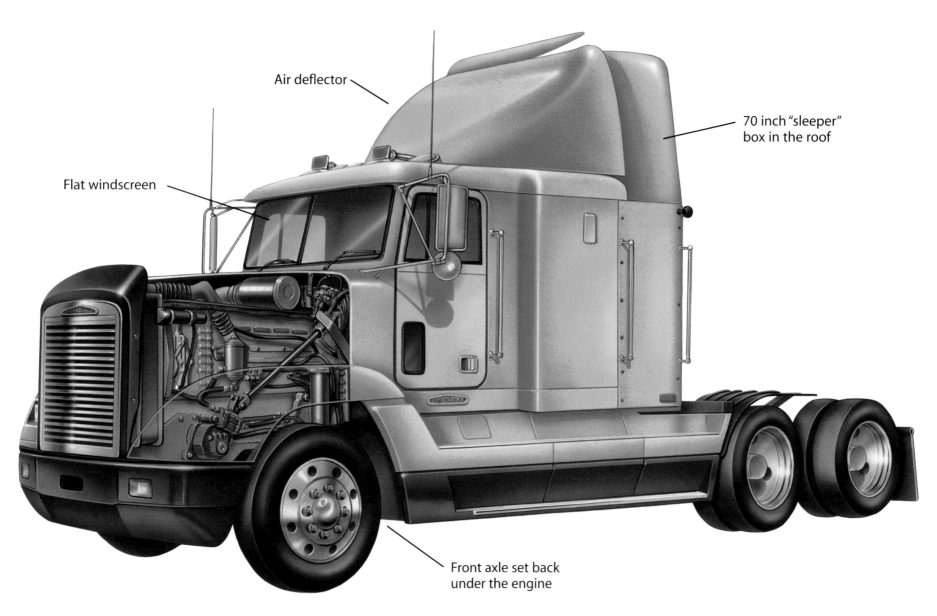

Air deflector

70 inch "sleeper" box in the roof

Flat windscreen

Front axle set back under the engine

Freightliner was founded by Leland James in 1939. James had been in the trucking business since the age of 19 and he saw a gap in the market. The trucks he built were large "box vans" made mainly of aluminum. Their lightweight design meant that a standard Freightliner could carry a ton more than most similar-size trucks. This edge meant that by the 1980s Freightliner had become one of America's largest heavy-duty truck producers, with models such as the FLD120 keeping the company's reputation for innovative design alive.

• • • • • • • • • • • • • • • • • •

Definitions

box van: Tall-sided vans, usually with double or roller-style doors at the back. These are one of the commonest types of van used for short to medium range deliveries.

• • • • • • • • • • • • • • • • • •

Truckers on the Citizens' Band

ABOVE: All regular Citizen's Band radio users have a "handle" (or call sign), which is a nickname that identifies them to other listeners.

ABOVE: A Century Class Freightliner, top-of-the-range in 1998.

Get Your Ears On!

Long before mobile phones or Internet chatrooms, people used CB radios to stay in touch while they were on the move. "CB," which means Citizen's Band radio, started out as a way for police officers to communicate with one another while they were out on the beat. By the 1970s, around 50 million

Did You Know?

The first Freightliners were given the nickname "Monkey Ward" because of their basic-looking design.

ordinary Americans were using CB as a fun way of communicating. For truckers, it was a great new tool. They could check with other drivers what the weather or road conditions ahead were like. They could transmit requests for help to the police or ambulance services. Most of all, though, it was a way to make friends and fight off boredom during long-distance journeys. All CB conversations are on an "open channel," so anyone can join in, but there are strict rules banning bad language, or people who jam the channel with music or endless chatter! Truckers even have their own CB phrases such as "ten-four" (which means, yes, I can hear you OK), "good buddy," and "read me" (hear my message).

75

IVECO EUROTECH

Curtainsider design
allows for easy loading
and unloading.

Roof sleeper box

The Eurotech has a carrying
capacity of 17 to 28 tons.

Powerful front disk brakes

The Euro series formed part of Iveco's family of heavy-duty trucks. These medium to heavy machines came with a choice of two cab styles, 300–514 hp engines, and a load-carrying capacity ranging from six to 48 tons. With these new models, the Italian-born company, which had been founded by Fiat in the 1970s, finally took its place as one of Europe's major truck manufacturers.

Did You Know?

Iveco stands for Industrial Vehicle Corporation. During its short life, Iveco has been involved in takeovers and partnerships with German truck manufacturer Magirus-Deutz, Spain's Pegaso, Britain's Seddon Atkinson, and Ford.

Knights of the Road

There's something romantic about the idea of a truck driver roaring off into the sunset in a huge, shiny "rig" with just the crackle of the CB radio for company. In popular culture, the trucker is the modern equivalent of the cowboy of old—an image that has been encouraged by movies and popular songs. During the 1970s and '80s, TV series like *BJ and the Bear,* and movies such as *Smokey and the Bandit* and *Every Which Way but Loose* (right) portrayed truckers as hard-living loners with their own tough but fair rules. In truckin' songs such as "Breaker Breaker" and "Convoy," truck drivers were men who lived outside of the law, and this made them cool. The truth, of

course, is less exciting. Most truckers aren't Clint Eastwood or Burt Reynolds, although some would like us to think so! However, at least part of the image is true. Channel 9 is the CB radio emergency frequency, and is always monitored by drivers, who pass on any calls for help to the police—which makes them true "knights of the road."

Definitions

sleeper box: A sleeping area that is connected to the driver's cab. These are often detachable.

rig: Another word for an articulated truck. The word developed from the name for a horse-drawn carriage.

MAN F2000

Disk and drum brakes. By law, all trucks must have a secondary braking system.

Air suspension available on all weight classes

Lightweight forged aluminum wheel centers

Flat "ladder-type" chassis frame

When it was launched, the F2000 series was the most powerful production truck in Europe, with a carrying capacity of 20–52 tons and a 270–600 bhp engine. Yet, there's more to the F2000 than just raw power. MAN has a well-established reputation for its practical and efficient designs, and the F2000 was built with not just driver comfort but safety and economy in mind.

Practical and Powerful

ABOVE: This MAN F2000 is equipped with a sleeper box and a curtainsider trailer.

Ahead of the Rest

MAN (short for Maschinenfabrik Augsburg-Nürnberg AG) has been at the forefront of truck technology since the start of the twentieth century. Like railroad engines, trucks began as steam-powered vehicles and MAN was one of Europe's earliest producers of steam engines.

By 1923, however, it was already experimenting with diesel power. The oil-burning engine, which was invented by Rudolf Diesel in 1892, is now a standard feature on most trucks, but MAN was the first company to offer the option of a diesel-powered vehicle rather than the standard gas-run model.

In 1951, it scored another first by developing a powerful, superefficient "turbo-charged" diesel. Its cutting-edge designs have, in fact, led to MAN winning the Truck of the Year award four times running. Today, one of the company's major concerns is to make its vehicles more environmentally friendly. It is already producing a range of buses powered by natural gas, and in 1995, a specially adapted 44-ton F2000 won the worldwide Eco-Challenge Tour. With such an active research and development team, it's likely that MAN will be staying well ahead of the competition for many years to come.

Did You Know?

By fitting a type of filter called a "catalytic converter" to its F2000 range, MAN was able to reduce the amount of poisonous gases that are released into the air in exhaust fumes by around 70 percent.

Definitions
ladder chassis: Basic trucks are built around a frame, made from steel or aluminum, called a ladder. The trailer and cab are fixed to this frame.

DAF 95XF SUPER SPACE CAB

Easy-to-handle small (17.7 inch) steering wheel

Spacious and comfortable cab design

"Four-point" cab suspension, including rear dampers for a gentler ride

The Van Dooren Trailer Factory, or "DAF," was the brainchild of brothers Hubertus and Wim van Doorne. From the beginning, it was DAF's designs that set it apart from its rivals. For example, its first truck, called the Daflosser, was fitted with a tilting platform that enabled goods to be easily loaded and unloaded. Sadly, DAF's fortunes have declined since the 1980s, but the flagship 95XF, produced in 1997 under the PACCAR name, is a reminder of just how good truck design can be.

Inside the Engine

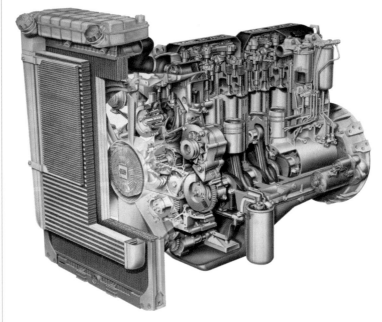

ABOVE: At the heart of the 95XF is a huge 12.6 liter (769 ci) DAF-built engine.

Military Machines

With such a flair for design, it wasn't surprising that DAF's work was soon noticed by the Dutch government, and by the 1950s over half of the company's vehicles were destined for the military. These vehicles may have looked more basic than DAF's civilian models, but they were still just as innovative.

The YA 616, for instance, came as a standard truck, tipper, or crane. The YP 408 was just as flexible. On the outside, this was just a chunky armored personnel carrier, but under its tough metal shell, it had lots of extras. An engine-driven air compressor, for example, was used to power the brakes. This could be adapted to inflate the vehicle's tires. Although the YP 408 wasn't truly amphibious, the engine's ventilation system could be sealed so that the truck could be driven through rivers up to a depth of 3 feet 11 inches. The 408 could also be used as a radio truck or an ambulance.

ABOVE: Like other truck manufacturers, such as Renault, DAF also produced a wide range of military vehicles such as this personnel carrier.

Did You Know?

Hubertus van Doorne was born in America, which is a small village in Holland.

RENAULT AE-SERIES 500 (1990)

High roof gives the driver more space to move about.

Aerodynamic "spoilers" reduce drag.

Shaped seats for additional comfort

Large windscreen

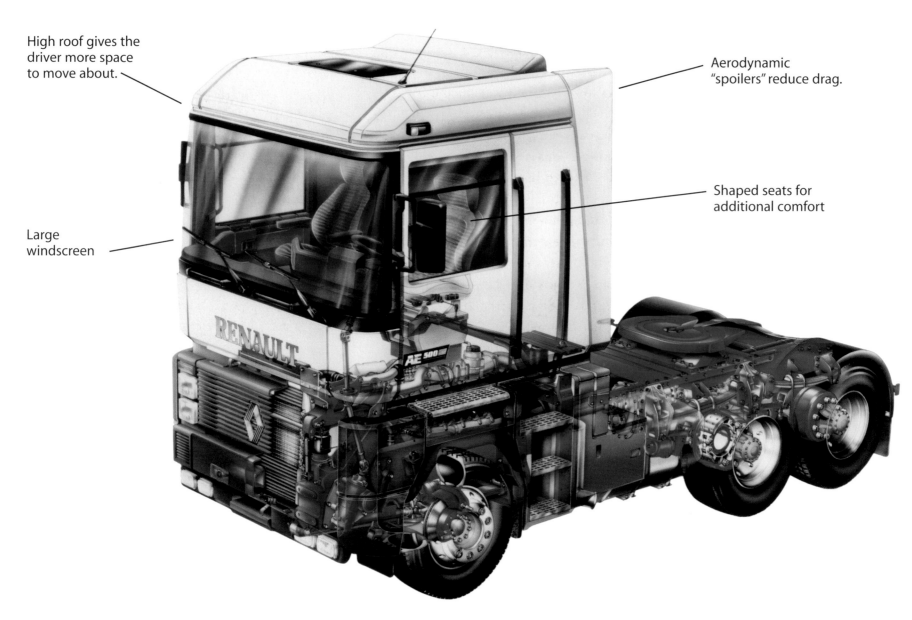

Just like tractors, trucks are machines designed for work, not play. This may be why so little attention has been given to the comfort of the driver during the last 100 years! Although great steps in cab design had been made by companies such as DAF, it was a French manufacturer, Renault, that really began to address the needs of long-distance drivers. And that's one of the reasons why the AE series was voted Truck of the Year in 1991.

French Fashion

Renault was founded in 1898 to build cars, but over the last century it has become just as famous for its tractors, military vehicles, high-performance racing cars, and family sedans. Like all successful business ventures, Renault has had its fair share of luck, but what's made this company stand out from the crowd may be its unique sense of style. Its earliest trucks, made in the 1920s, were nicknamed coal scuttles because of the unique shape of the hood. The cars benefited from the same unique Renault styling too. Even the Ares 735RZ tractor pictured below is immediately recognizable as a Renault. It may be a powerful workhorse, but it's the quirky, rounded hood and the huge floor-to-ceiling windows in the farmer's cab that most people notice first.

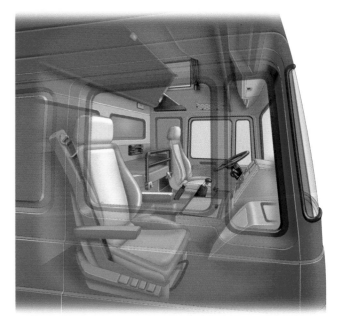

It's Great to Be Single!

ABOVE: This illustration shows the interior of Renault's Premium Single cab, which was produced in 1998. If the AE Series cabs were comfortable, the Single Cabs were luxurious! Inside, there is enough headroom for the driver to stand up straight. The sleeper boxes came with air conditioning and an optional refrigerator!

MACK MILLENNIUM SLEEPER CH SERIES

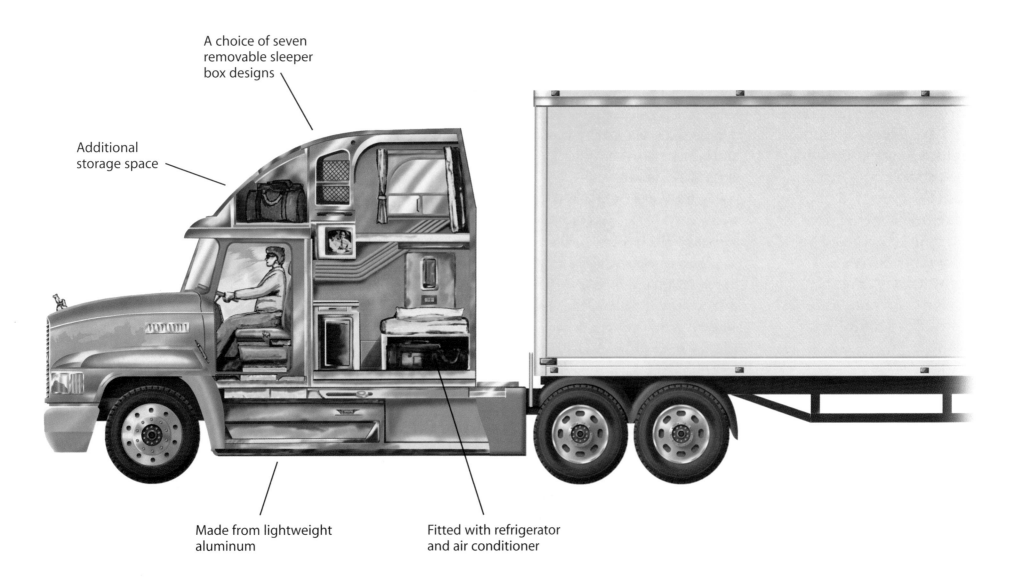

A choice of seven
removable sleeper
box designs

Additional
storage space

Made from lightweight
aluminum

Fitted with refrigerator
and air conditioner

Although Mack is now part of Renault (see pages 82–83), its trucks retain a distinctly American look. In fact, the Mack Millennium Sleeper was designed specifically to meet the needs of U.S. haulers, who tend to travel much longer distances than their European cousins. Today's CH Series come with specially designed sleeper boxes, which are insulated to reduce outside noise, and can be kept at a constant temperature of 68°F. These, plus a range of other comforts, make the Millennium Sleeper a real home away from home.

Did You Know?

During World War I, British soldiers nicknamed Mack's AC truck "the Bulldog" after an especially tough breed of English dog. Mack later adopted the bulldog as the company's logo.

Clever Cabs

Truck manufacturers have always had to balance the needs of the haulage company against the needs of the driver. However, there are strict rules governing the size and weight of trucks, so the bigger the driver's cab, or sleeping box, the less space there is for the load. Today's drivers are demanding greater comfort, and not just when curling up in their sleeper compartment at the end of a day. Manufacturers have had to respond, and the images below show how Mercedes-Benz has tackled the problem. It has developed a range of cabs that offer maximum driver comfort, whatever the type of journey. The S Cab is the smallest of the range, and is intended for short journeys only. The M Cab is for medium journeys and includes a folding bunk. The L Cab and Megaspace are both long-haul designs. The Megaspace is high enough to let the driver stand completely upright inside.

S Cab for short journeys

M Cab includes folding bunk

L Cab—a long-haul design

VOLVO FH GLOBETROTTER SERIES

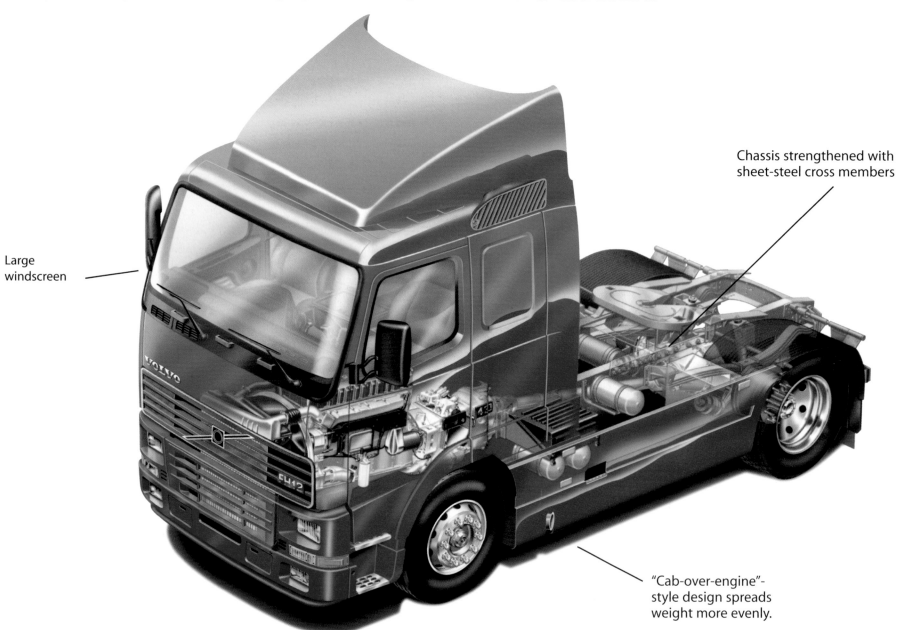

Chassis strengthened with
sheet-steel cross members

Large
windscreen

"Cab-over-engine"-
style design spreads
weight more evenly.

By the 1990s, the heavy-duty Globetrotter range had become one of Volvo's most successful trucks ever. The reason for its popularity was twofold. First, the range was incredibly flexible. It came in truck-trailer models and semitrailers, as well as construction vehicles and rigs designed for long-distance haulage. The second reason was its new, exceptionally powerful engine, pictured at right.

Power and Performance

ABOVE: The power behind the FH series was the new DC12C engine, which Volvo also fitted to its American White/GMC branded vehicles. This made the FH series capable of around 460 hp.

plugs, and takes place inside the cylinders. A piston inside the cylinder sucks in fuel and air as it moves up. When it reaches the top of the cylinder, it hits a spark plug, which ignites the fuel. The burning gases then push the piston down, which powers the engine.

The second type of engine is called a "compression-ignition" engine. When air is put under pressure, or compressed, by the pistons in the cylinder, it heats up. If the air gets hot enough, it will immediately "combust" when fuel is added to the mix. Compression-ignition engines usually use diesel as a fuel, and so are often called diesel engines. Diesel is less processed than gas, so it is cheaper. It can also burn at a lower temperature than gas, meaning the engine can do more work before overheating. This makes it ideal for vehicles designed for heavy work, like trucks, tractors, and buses.

Did You Know?

Many of Volvo's truck models carry the letters "LV." This stands for Lastvagen, which means truck in Swedish.

Why Use Diesel?

Two main types of combustion engines are used in vehicles. The first is called a spark-ignition engine, where the power comes from the "combustion" (burning) of air and gas. The combustion is caused by sparks from the spark

CHAPTER FIVE

Heavy Equipment

From giant excavators and tunnelers to powerful bulldozers, dump trucks, and road rollers, heavy equipment makes construction work look like child's play.

It's amazing to think that when the ancient Egyptians built the pyramids, they did it without any machinery. Right up until the middle of the nineteenth century, if you wanted to build, dig, lift, push, or pull a load, the only labor-saving devices available to make the job easier were simple pulleys and levers. Incredible feats of engineering such as the Brooklyn Bridge were completed by laborers using simple tools very similar to those their ancestors had used thousands of years before. All that changed with the invention of the combustion engine. With it came hundreds of specialist machines, all designed to make the job of demolition and construction a lot easier.

BUCYRUS-ERIE 1550-W WALKING DRAGLINE

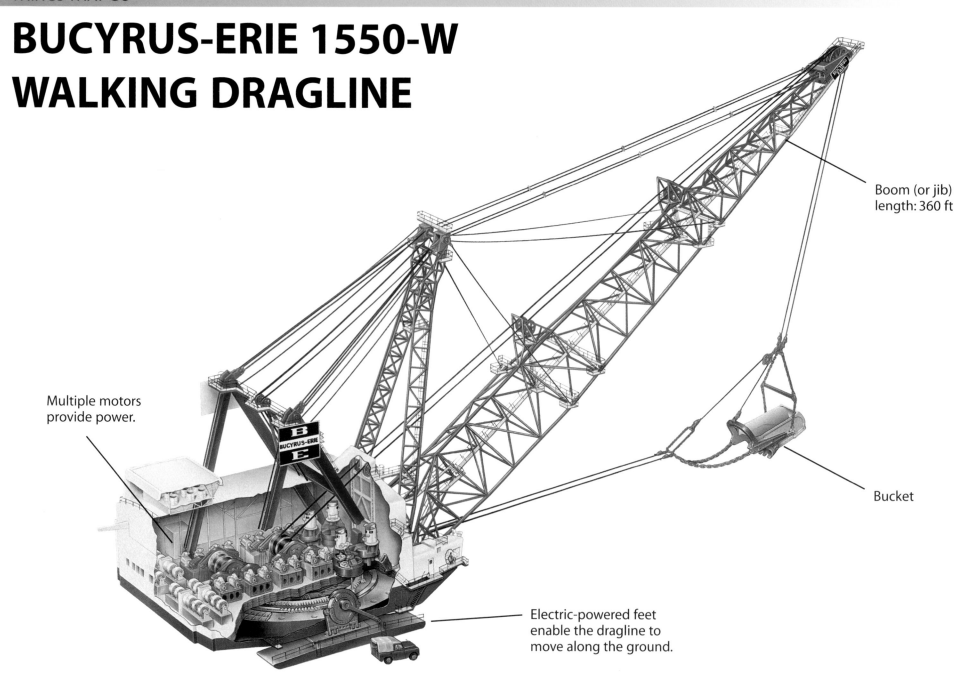

Boom (or jib) length: 360 ft

Multiple motors provide power.

Bucket

Electric-powered feet enable the dragline to move along the ground.

In the world of big diggers, you don't get much larger than Bucyrus-Erie's 1550-W "walking dragline," nicknamed "Big George." This huge machine is really just a complex system of hoists and pulleys, powered by electric engines. Designed to strip the earth from the surface of open-cast mines, Big George's bucket can carry the equivalent of a couple of family cars in every journey. Machines like Big George are so huge that they have to be built on site and then dismantled once the job is done.

Did You Know?

The biggest piece of construction equipment in the world was a 330-ton-capacity Bucyrus-Erie 4250-W walking dragline excavator, which was affectionately known as "Big Muskie." It took three years to build and cost $25 million.

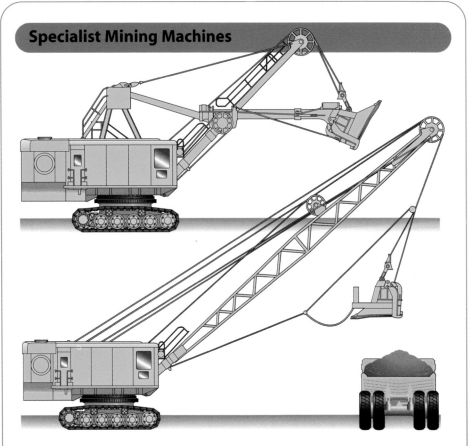

Specialist Mining Machines

Excavators are powered digging machines. The mining shovel (top) digs up earth, while draglines drag it out as the bucket is pulled toward the operator with a cable attached to a long boom. Mining shovels have now been replaced by hydraulically powered excavators (see page 99). But the dragline (bottom) is still used. Once the bucket is filled, the operator "slews," or swings, the excavator around and dumps the earth.

What Is a Walking Dragline?

Draglines were developed around 1903 in Chicago. These early steam-powered versions of today's huge machines were often positioned on the back of railroad trucks and used to cut canals. The dragline would be moved along the railroad track as the job progressed. Walking draglines, like Big George, have two huge electric-powered feet, which can be lifted slowly up and down. These spread the weight more effectively than caterpillar tracks, and stop the heavy machine from sinking into the ground. These "feet" are very slow, though. In fact, the dragline doesn't really walk at all, it just shuffles!

CATERPILLAR D10 BULLDOZER

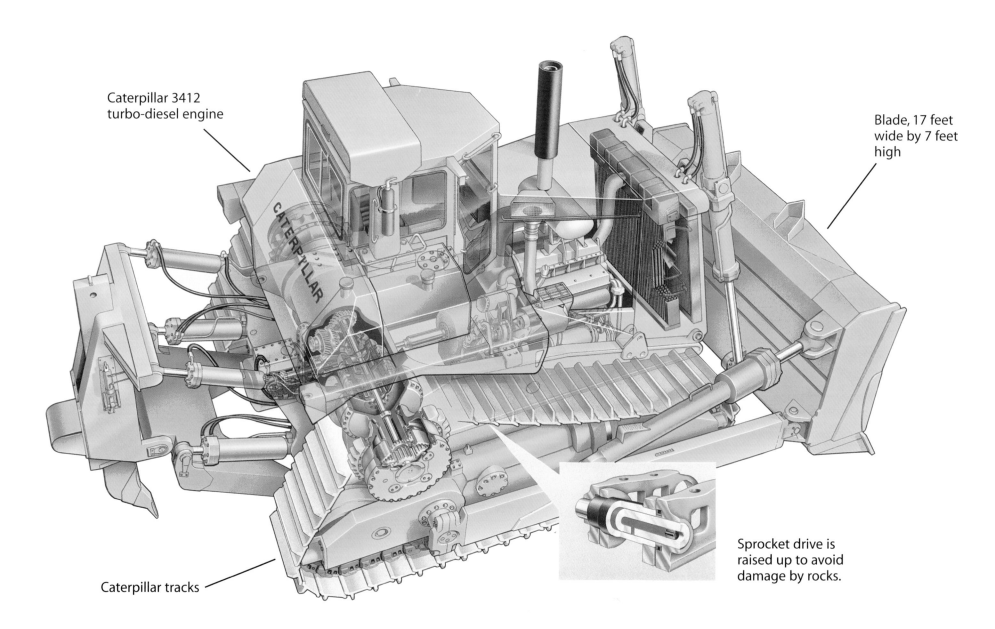

Caterpillar 3412
turbo-diesel engine

Blade, 17 feet
wide by 7 feet
high

Caterpillar tracks

Sprocket drive is
raised up to avoid
damage by rocks.

Caterpillar is one of the world's most successful manufacturers of track-driven vehicles. With a distinctive Highway Yellow color scheme and bold CAT logo, they are a familiar sight on farms (see pages 66–67) and have even launched a clothing brand, but they're relative newcomers to the world of construction. The D10 bulldozer was first produced in 1977, and it was a sensation. Beneath the heavy metal yellow shell was a revolutionary new "sprocket drive," which dramatically reduced wear on the bulldozer's moving parts.

The Right Tools for the Job

BELOW: Part of the appeal of the bulldozer is that different blades can be attached to the machine to suit the job. This Liebherr PR752 bulldozer is fitted with a lightweight blade, designed to handle topsoil.

'Dozer Development

Bulldozers were born during World War I, when designers were experimenting with tracked vehicles like tanks. It was discovered that by fitting a blade onto the front of an armored truck or tank, the weight of the vehicle could be used to push obstructions and earth out of the way. Today, bulldozers come in all shapes and sizes, but the basic design has stayed the same. A bulldozer is really just a crawler tractor with a large blade attached to the front. Like wheeled loaders (pages 100–101) and hydraulic excavators (pages 94–95) they're used primarily to move earth, although they tend to "push" rather than "scoop." However, it's their maneuverability and flexibility that has made them one of the construction industry's most useful tools. This is all thanks to their tracks. Wheeled 'dozers do exist, but those with tracks have remained popular because they help to spread out the vehicle's weight so that it doesn't sink. This has proved to be extremely useful in environments like construction sites, where heavy vehicles have to cope with muddy and uneven ground.

LIEBHERR R984B EXCAVATOR

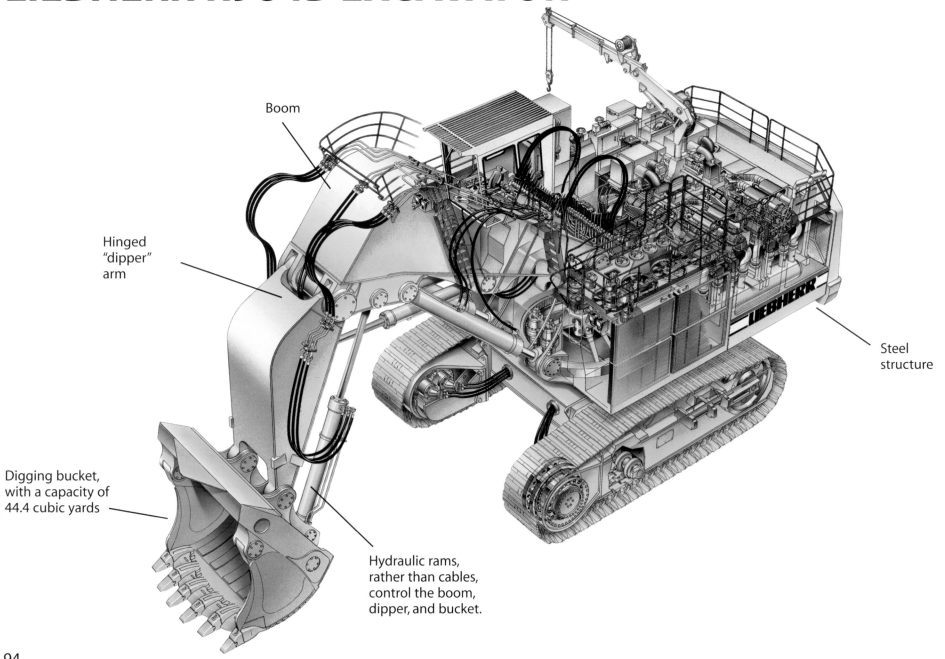

Boom

Hinged "dipper" arm

Steel structure

Digging bucket, with a capacity of 44.4 cubic yards

Hydraulic rams, rather than cables, control the boom, dipper, and bucket.

The Liebherr family has been in the business of building big machines for 55 years. They're now one of the leading manufacturers of construction machinery, thanks to crawler excavators like the R984B. This compact vehicle is used in open-cast mines around the world, especially in diamond digging operations in South Africa, where it's used to strip off overburden and load gravel into dump trucks. With specialized attachments available, this is one of Liebherr's most popular and versatile vehicles.

Definitions

open-cast: Mines in which the material is close enough to the surface to be dug out without sinking a mine shaft.
overburden: The layer of rock or soil that covers seams of coal, or other minerals.
clamshell: Dredging bucket, used to remove gravel from river beads, which is hinged like the shell of a clam.
auger: A tool shaped like a corkscrew, used to bore holes.

Did You Know?

Liebherr was established by Hans Liebherr in 1949 and is still owned by the family.

All Change!

Modern construction firms prefer crawler excavators to larger mining shovels because they're more accurate, can be easily moved, and are readily adapted to take on a range of jobs. On most excavators and wheeled loaders, the bucket is attached to the dipper arm. This in turn is attached to the boom, or jib. Generally, all buckets can be changed to suit the needs of the operator, and models such as the R984B come with an extensive range of buckets and clamshells as well as hammers and augers. These illustrations show a selection of available bucket designs. On the left is a lean-up bucket, which can easily be emptied. Next is a frost bucket, which is fitted with large teeth to cut through ice. The third illustration shows a twist bucket, which can be tilted 45 degrees in either direction. The final example is a chuck blade. This is used to scrape rather than dig earth, and is especially useful at clearing ditches.

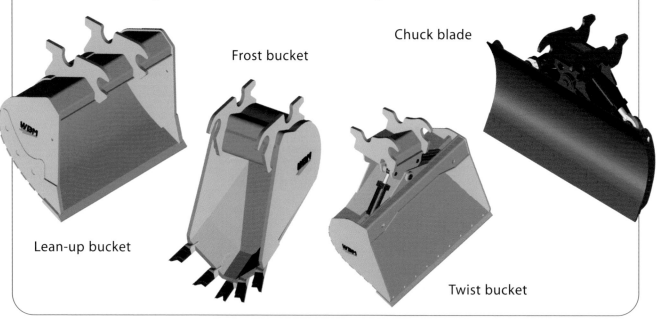

Chuck blade

Frost bucket

Lean-up bucket

Twist bucket

ROBBINS TBM-529 FULL-FACE BORER

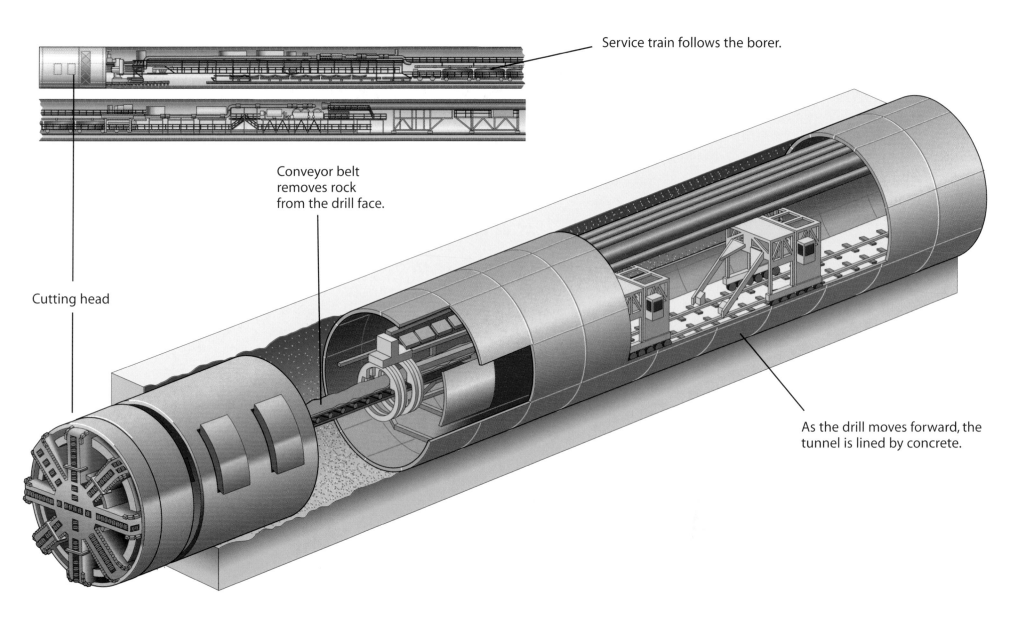

Service train follows the borer.

Conveyor belt removes rock from the drill face.

Cutting head

As the drill moves forward, the tunnel is lined by concrete.

Fifty years ago, an engineer working for a firm called Robbins made one of the most important breakthroughs in tunnel construction. He discovered that if you put a spinning metal wheel with a sharp cutting face against a rock's surface, it will cut through the rock as long as there's enough pressure behind the wheel. Today, Robbins remains at the forefront of TBM construction and design, with extraordinary machines such as the 529, which was built in 1974.

Did You Know?

The first tunnel borer produced by Robbins was called the Mittry Mole, after F.K. Mittry, who designed it. It was used during the construction of the Oahe Dam in South Dakota.

Cutting-Edge Machinery!

Early TBMs (Tunnel Boring Machines) were slow, expensive, and unreliable, which is why many tunnelers stuck to the old "drill and blast" method, which used explosives to blow holes in the rock. Today's modern TBMs, though, can slice through up to 20 feet of rock an hour in any direction. This photo shows the rotating cutter head of one of the full-face tunnel borers used during the construction of the Channel Tunnel between England and France. Eventually 11 of these huge machines were used, and the total job cost a staggering $15 billion.

Tunnel Under the Sea

Just 22 miles of sea separate Britain from France, and the idea of connecting the two countries with a tunnel has been discussed for centuries. The French emperor Napoleon was supposed to have started building a tunnel to invade Britain during the 1800s. Adolf Hitler was rumored to have done the same in the 1940s. However, the first real attempts to build a tunnel were made in 1875, when J.D. Burton constructed the world's first full-face boring machine to do the job. Unfortunately, it simply wasn't powerful enough. England and France had to wait until 1991 for tunnelers, digging from both ends, to finally meet, 140 feet beneath the waters of the English Channel. The illustration on page 96 shows just one of the three tunnels that were constructed. (There were two railroad tunnels and one service tunnel.)

INTERNATIONAL 3500 TRACTOR LOADER

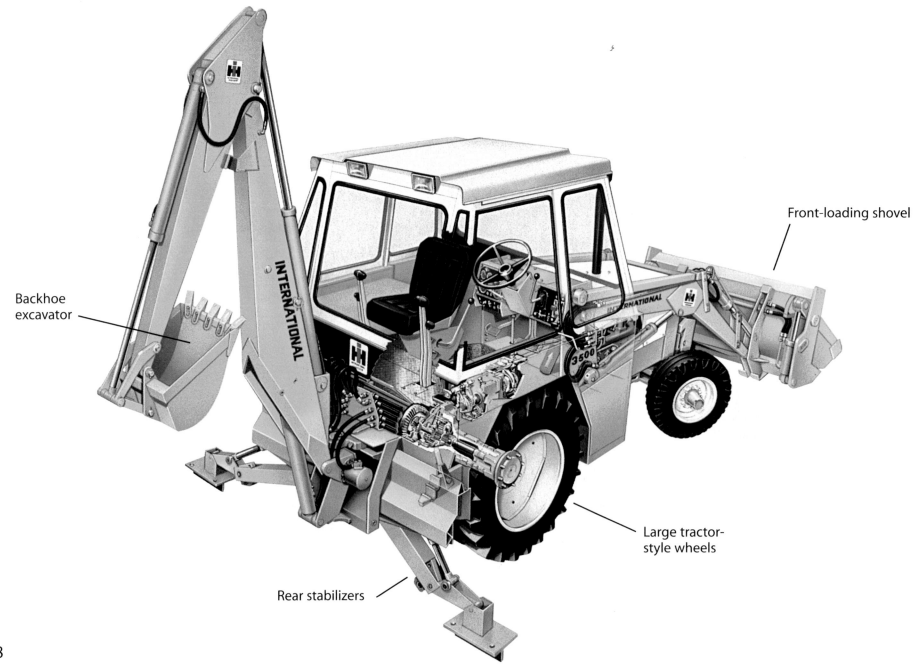

Front-loading shovel

Backhoe
excavator

Large tractor-
style wheels

Rear stabilizers

In the construction industry, terminology can be tricky. If you hear a construction worker talking about loaders, it's likely that he means one of two types of vehicles. The first is a wheeled loader (see pages 100–101); the second is a tractor loader. Tractor loaders are one of the most widely used construction vehicles. The name comes from its dual heritage—it's part tractor and part loader.

Did You Know?

Although popular, some hydraulic vehicles are actually less hard-wearing than cable-powered machines. In fact, cable excavators have been known to outlast the mine that they were built to work in!

Definitions

backhoe: The name for the bucket mounted on a boom at the back of a tractor excavator, or the front of a loader.

Hydraulics in Action

ABOVE: Hydraulically operated machinery has its origins in experiments carried out by W.G. Armstrong in the 1880s. Most manufacturers now produce a wide range of hydraulic excavators and loaders.

How Hydraulics Work

Machines such as draglines are cable-powered. The bucket moves when the cables attached to it are winched up and down by electric motors. Draglines are useful in construction because they're able to move vast quantities of earth. Mining shovels, which are smaller, also use cables, but have now mostly been replaced by hydraulic excavators and loaders, which are more maneuverable. Rams, rather than cables, control the movement of the boom, dipper, and bucket. They do this using hydraulics. When you put water or another liquid into a small space like a tube, and apply pressure to it, it does not become compressed like the air in a balloon. Instead, the liquid resists the pressure—unless it is released. By applying pressure to a large area, and allowing this pressure to escape only through a small hole (just like a water pistol), powerful forces can be achieved that can move rocks and other heavy materials. Hydraulic machines are used throughout the construction industry, especially to lift heavy loads, but the same principles have been adapted for hydraulic presses, brakes, and power steering in cars.

JCB 456B ZX WHEELED LOADER

Engine over rear axle acts as a counter-balance to the weight of the bucket.

Powerful hydraulic rams

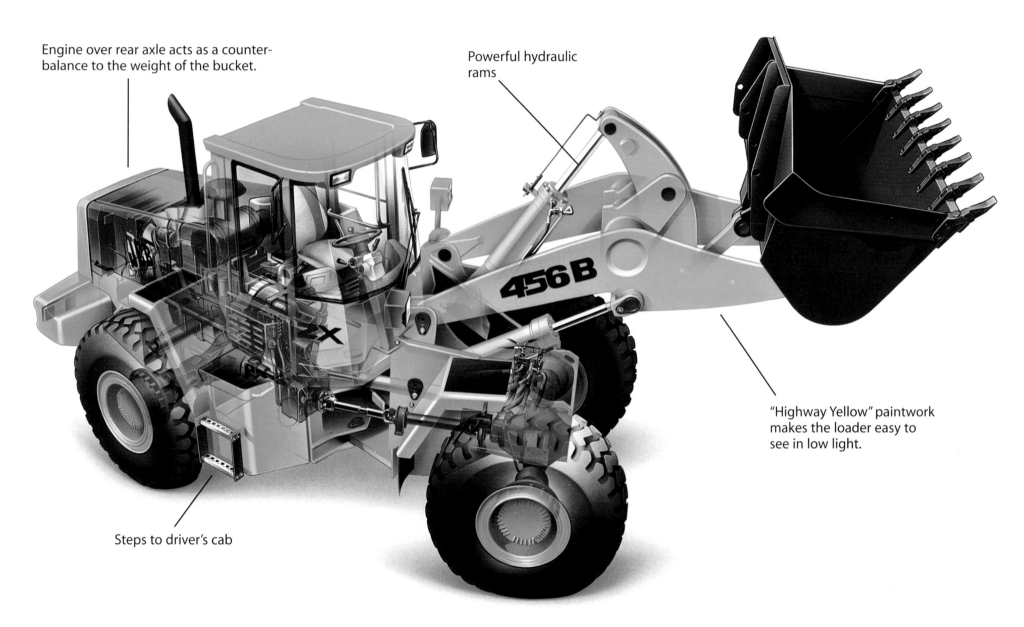

"Highway Yellow" paintwork makes the loader easy to see in low light.

Steps to driver's cab

Sixty years after Joseph Cyril Bamford started his construction and farm equipment business, JCB has become a world-famous brand that employs over 4,000 people in four continents. Its range of heavy equipment includes over 160 different models, from the famous tractor loaders to excavators and wheeled loaders. When it appeared in 1998, the 456B gave drivers new levels of comfort, control, and economy.

ABOVE: Four-wheel drive is also popular in cars.

Did You Know?

When Joseph Cyril Bamford started his business, he worked out of a garage that measured just 12 x 15 feet.

Scoop and Dump

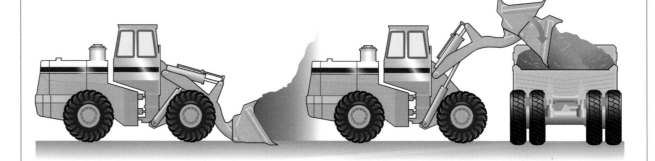

To scoop up and unload earth into a dump truck is a simple three-part process. First the bucket, in the down position, is filled. Hydraulically powered rams then move the boom and dipper arm until the bucket is in the correct position for unloading. Finally, the bucket is tipped over so that the contents can be taken away.

What Is Four-Wheel Drive?

In the past, driving and steering were split between the front and back axles. The axles are the bars to which the wheels of a vehicle are attached. The power from the engine was used to move (or drive) the back wheels, and you turned the steering wheel to move the front wheels in the direction you wanted to go. In the 1970s, manufacturers combined the drive and steering functions into one. These "front-wheel-drive" vehicles were lighter and therefore more fuel efficient. But all the power goes to the front wheels, so there's less grip at the back, making control difficult at high speeds. In a four-wheeled vehicle with four-wheel drive, the engine's power is shared between the front and back axles, for more control. This is good for tractors or excavators, which often drive on uneven road surfaces. In a four-wheel-drive six-wheeler, the engine powers just four of the wheels.

TEREX 4066C ADT DUMP TRUCK

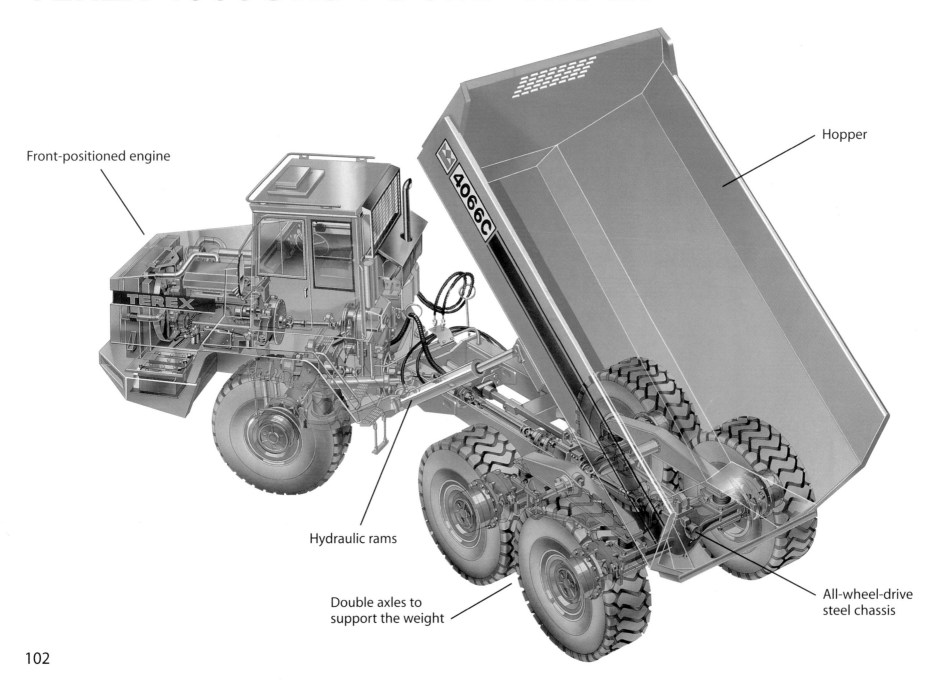

Front-positioned engine

Hopper

Hydraulic rams

Double axles to
support the weight

All-wheel-drive
steel chassis

Dump trucks seem to be one of the most basic of construction vehicles. After all, they don't have anything clever like tracks or electronic winches. Yet, as this diagram shows, there's more to a dump truck than meets the eye. The 4066C is an "articulated" dump truck (ADT). At the front is a tractor-style cab. At the back is a hopper, which can be lifted up and down by hydraulic rams (see page 99). The whole is held together by an all-wheel-drive (6 x 6), steel chassis. All that adds up to a lot of technical know-how.

Did You Know?

Dumper trucks were probably used for the first time during the construction of the Hoover Dam.

Getting the Balance Right

In construction vehicles, it's important to balance the weight of the load against the weight of the vehicle; otherwise, a fully loaded bucket will pull a truck over. In loaders, where the bucket is at the front, the engine is toward the back. Tractor loaders, like the International 3500, have buckets at the front and rear, so the engine is placed in the middle. In a dump truck, once the hopper is tipped up, all the weight is at the back, so the engine is as close to the front of the vehicle as possible to balance things out.

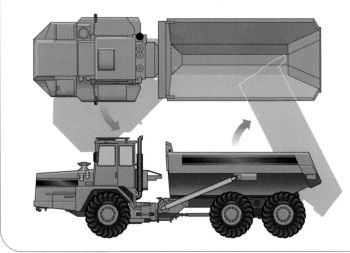

Definitions
articulated: Made up of a number of sections joined together.

Dumper Design

Dump truck designs vary depending on the jobs they do. Those intended to carry heavy loads, like rock, have low sides, to stop the truck being overloaded. High-sided dumpers are used for lighter loads. This photo shows a Moxy MT36. Some dump trucks are "rigids," but the MT36 is an "articulated" dump truck. Here the driver's cab is attached to the hopper by a flexible arm, which gives it more maneuverability on uneven surfaces. At the heart of the dump truck are hydraulic rams, which lift the hopper up to empty out the load. However, not all dump trucks work like this. Some, called "bottom dump" trucks, have a door on the bottom of the hopper. These open like bomb-bay doors when the load needs to be released.

103

AVELING-BARFORD HDC12 ROLLER

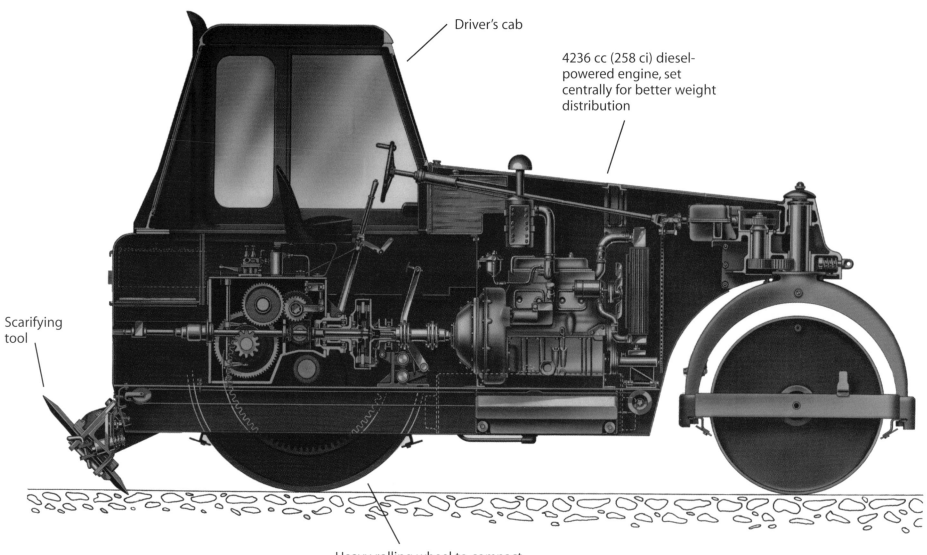

Driver's cab

4236 cc (258 ci) diesel-powered engine, set centrally for better weight distribution

Scarifying tool

Heavy rolling wheel to compact (press down) the earth

British farmer and engineer Thomas Aveling is one of the key figures in the development of modern-day road-building equipment. His first successful steam-powered roller, which was designed to crush down the layers of the road's surface, was made in 1873. This illustration shows an Aveling-Barford model HDC12 diesel-powered roller, which still carries Thomas Aveling's name a remarkable 131 years later!

● ● ● ● ● ● ● ● ● ● ● ● ● ● ● ● ● ●

Definitions
scarifying: To break up or loosen soil.

● ● ● ● ● ● ● ● ● ● ● ● ● ● ● ● ● ●

Did You Know?

The standard width for a Roman road was just under five feet. This is about the same as the width of a modern railroad track.

Rolling Along

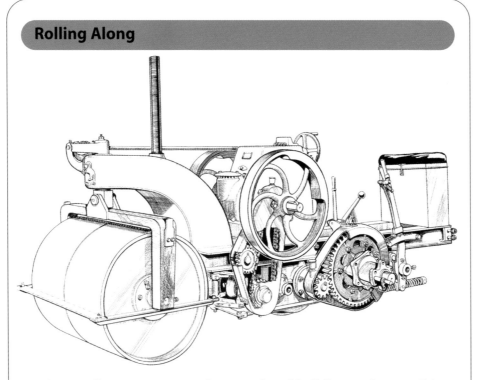

ABOVE: Aveling & Porter were pioneers of road-building equipment. This illustration shows an Aveling & Porter diesel-powered roller from 1927. The design is not that different from the HDC12, built in 1991.

Then and Now

The Roman Empire—the super-power of the ancient world—was the first large-scale road builder. The technique was simple, but hard work. The road's footings were built first, usually a layer of rubble for good water drainage. On top were placed layers of ever finer material, pressed down well. The

top layer was paved or covered in another layer of fine stone. These roads always had a "camber," which means that they were curved so rain ran down into drainage ditches at either side of the road. Modern European roads (above) often use the same routes and a similar "layering" technique. Their design varies, but the bottom layer, called the roadbed, is usually made of earth that has been leveled by excavators. The second layer is the base course, made of compacted (crushed down) gravel. The final layer is the wearing course, made of bitumen or concrete. Thankfully, much of the work can be done with construction vehicles like the HDC12.

GOMACO GP4000 PAVER

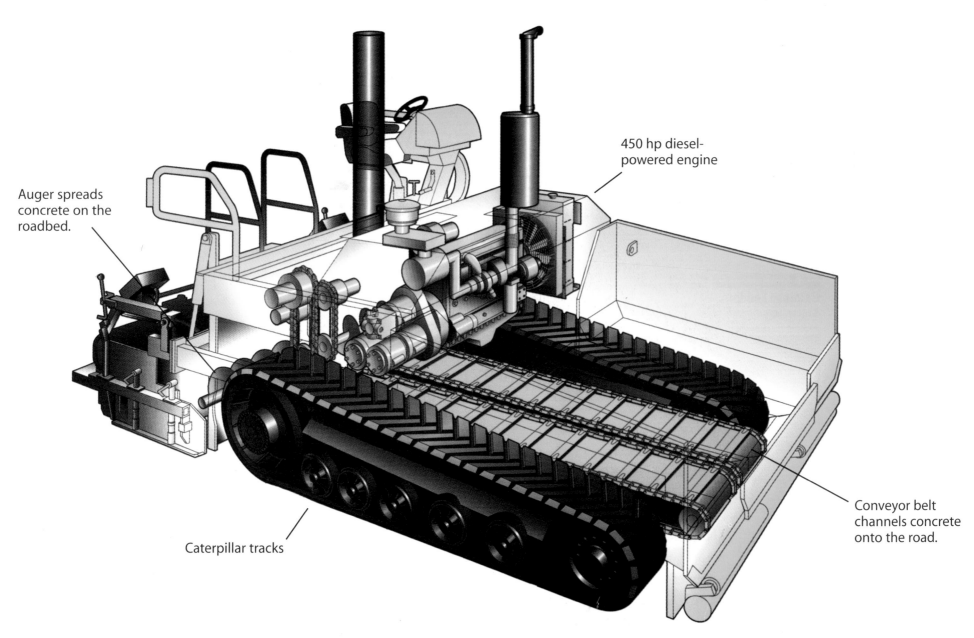

450 hp diesel-powered engine

Auger spreads concrete on the roadbed.

Conveyor belt channels concrete onto the road.

Caterpillar tracks

Once the road surface has been prepared using excavators, loaders, dump trucks, and rollers, it's time for the Gomaco GP4000 to step in. Huge paving vehicles like this were built to lay down the wearing course, which is the topmost layer of the road. New road-building machines are being developed all the time, but when it was built in 1997, this 44-ton monster could spread a layer of concrete 18 inches deep and 50 feet wide.

ABOVE: A Gomaco trimmer at work on a new road-building project.

Tons of Concrete!

ABOVE: Twenty-first-century construction uses vast quantities of concrete.

It's All in the Mix

The Romans were great engineers and builders, so it's no surprise that they knew all about concrete. It may seem like one of the most modern materials, but in fact the famous Colosseum in Rome was made, in A.D. 80, using concrete. The Romans even had their own recipe, which was described by Vitruvius in his *Ten Books of Architecture*. Basically, it consisted of two or three parts of sand for every one part of chalk, mixed with water. Modern concrete is a little more sophisticated, but the basic ingredients are the same. To make concrete, all you need is a filler and

a binder. The filler can be any solid material like sand or rock. This is all held together by the binder, cement. Cement is made by burning limestone (which is chemically similar to chalk) and clay at very high temperatures. Add water to the mix, and you have concrete. The strength of the finished concrete depends on what sort of material is used for the aggregate and how much cement is used.

CHAPTER SIX

Aircraft

Humans have dreamed about flying since they first looked up into the skies. From fighter planes to giant airliners, here are some of the most spectacular flying machines ever.

The first true controlled flights were by balloon, but it took another 100 years for humans to take to the air using engine power. These early attempts at getting airborne were inspired, ingenious, sometimes even brilliant, but more often than not just plain dangerous. Airplane designs powered by steam were tested and built in the 1890s. Some even flew—for a few seconds—but it was the Wright brothers whose work gave birth to modern heavier-than-air aircraft in 1903. Since then, airplane designers—and their brave test pilots— have presented us with ever faster, bigger, and more powerful machines to marvel at and enjoy.

SUPERMARINE SPITFIRE V

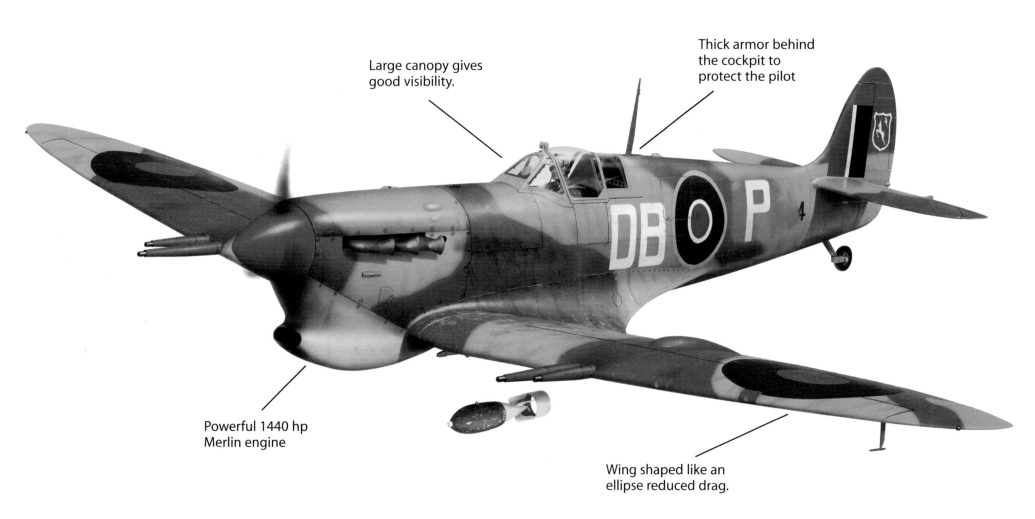

Large canopy gives
good visibility.

Thick armor behind
the cockpit to
protect the pilot

Powerful 1440 hp
Merlin engine

Wing shaped like an
ellipse reduced drag.

To Britons, the Spitfire is the airplane that will forever be associated with the Battle of Britain. Designed in the 1930s, this relatively small fighter owed much of its success to its elliptical wings and powerful Rolls-Royce Merlin 45 engines. Although technically slower than its common adversary, the Messerschmitt Bf 109, the plane was so maneuverable that it became the king of the air-to-air battle and a firm favorite with flyers and civilians alike.

Did You Know?

Spitfires took three times as long to manufacture as the Messerschmitt Bf 109.

Definitions
ellipse: Shape like a flattened circle.

The Battle of Britain

By 1940, Germany had seized control over much of mainland Europe, but Britain still refused to surrender. During the long hot summer that followed, the German Luftwaffe decided to take action. It launched an all-out aerial attack on the British mainland, hoping to knock out Britain's air force in preparation for an invasion across the narrow stretch of water that separated England from France. Over the next few months, although heavily outnumbered, Spitfires and Hurricanes of the Royal Air Force inflicted heavy losses on their opponents. It's estimated that around 1,700 German aircraft were lost to 900 British. In September, Germany switched tactics and began a series of heavy bombing raids on cities such as London and Liverpool, a campaign which became known as the Blitz. While this was a terrible time for Britain's civilian population, the threat of invasion had passed, and the RAF was able to rebuild its forces in preparation for a counterattack. Later, the British Prime Minister, Winston Churchill, echoed the thoughts of all Britons when he said: "The gratitude of every home in our island…goes out to the British airmen, who, undaunted by the odds, are turning the tide of world war by their prowess and devotion. Never in the field of human conflict was so much owed by so many to so few."

MESSERSCHMITT BF 109E

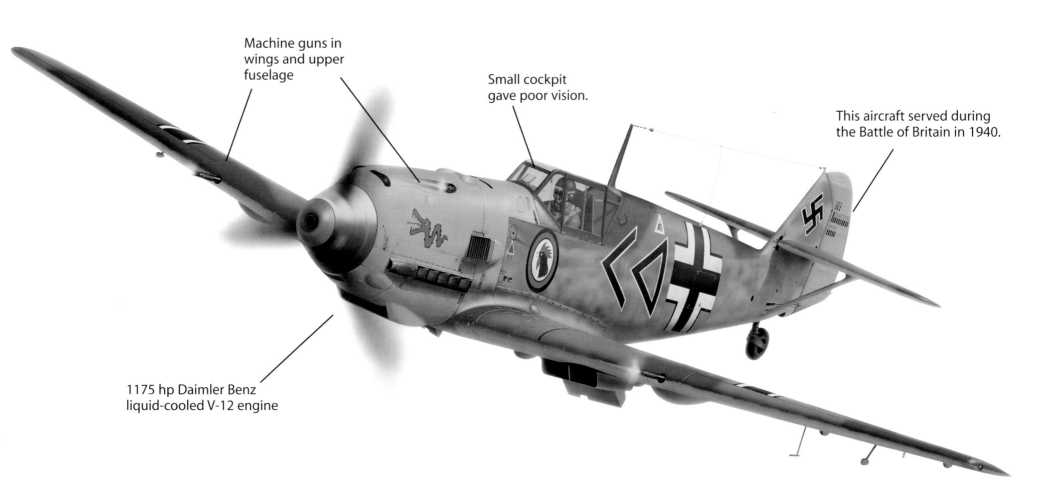

Machine guns in
wings and upper
fuselage

Small cockpit
gave poor vision.

This aircraft served during
the Battle of Britain in 1940.

1175 hp Daimler Benz
liquid-cooled V-12 engine

At the start of World War II, Germany's standard fighter was the single-seat Messerschmitt Bf 109. Numerous versions of this basic model were built, but the E series is still considered to be the finest. Fitted with four machine guns (two in the nose and two in the wings), and with a top speed of 348 mph, this could be a deadly weapon in the hands of an experienced German pilot.

Did You Know?

More than 4,000 Messerschmitts were built, the most celebrated model being the 109E-3, which was used extensively during the Battle of Britain.

Mounts of the Bf 109 Aces

ABOVE: Major William Balthasar won 40 aerial dogfights, and was awarded the Knight's Cross with Oak Leaves and Swords. He was killed in 1941 when his Bf 109 lost a wing.

ABOVE: During his amazing flying career, Heinz Bär notched up 221 victories, making him the 3rd-ranking fighter ace of the war. Bär was shot down 18 times, but lived to tell the tale every time.

ABOVE: Adolf Galland not only had 104 combat victories, but made many modifications to the design of the 109. These included additional armor, better weapons, and a cigar lighter in the cockpit!

Aces High

In the days before computer technology and ejector seats, fighter pilots had to rely on their skill in the air to keep themselves alive. In World War I, pilots such as Manfred Von Richthofen, known as the Red Baron, became known as aces because they brought down so many enemy planes. During World War II, pilots from all over the world proved themselves equally skilled. Top aces included flyers such as Germany's Erich Hartmann, who had 352 combat victories, Walter Nowotny of Austria (258), Hiroyoshi Nishizawa of Japan (103), and E.I. Juutualainen of Finland (94).

BOEING B-17G FLYING FORTRESS

Four 1200 hp Wright Cyclone engines

Room inside for a crew of up to ten

Up to 13 machine guns were in place to defend the plane. This included a gunner in the "ball turret" under the fuselage.

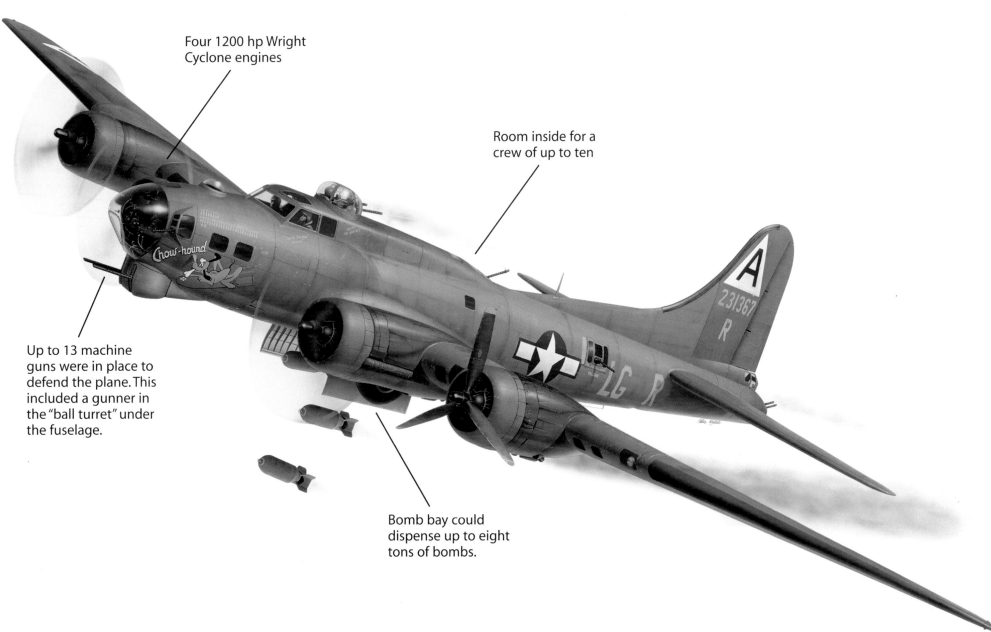

Bomb bay could dispense up to eight tons of bombs.

The Flying Fortress is probably one of the most famous planes of World War II. Several versions of this four-engined heavy bomber were built, but it's the B-17E, F, and G that have the distinctive "fat" body, chunky tail, and gun turret that we have all come to recognize from movies such as *Memphis Belle*. The B-17 played a vital role in the war in Europe. Over 12,000 of these great "silver birds" were built, and they formed the backbone of the U.S. Eighth Air Force.

Did You Know?

The B-17 was one of the first ever all-metal bombers.

Close-up Nose Art

ABOVE: One of the most distinctive features of USAF planes was that the pilots and crew were allowed to personalize them. Many were given names, often in memory of a sweetheart back home, or of cartoon characters such as "Chow-hound" pictured here.

The "Mighty Eighth"

At the height of World War II, B-17s could be found on almost every airfield in Britain. Just 22 miles from German-occupied France, Britain was the front line of the war in Europe and B-17s became a familiar sight, as did the pilots and crew of the "Mighty" Eighth Air Force, whose bravery and daring became legendary. Due to the difficulty of targeting accurately at night, the Mighty Eighth flew daylight bombing missions over heavily protected enemy territory. Bombers are heavy and relatively slow, which makes them an easy target for enemy fighters. Even a well-armored heavy bomber like the Flying Fortress had to be accompanied on its missions by an escort of fighter planes. Sadly, casualties were still high among bomber crews. More than 47,000 were killed in bombing missions, most of them young men in their teens and early twenties.

BOEING 337 STRATOCRUISER

The Stratocruiser had a very similar tail unit to the B-50 nuclear bomber.

Inside were sleeping berths, a lower-deck lounge bar, and a galley with electric ovens.

Power provided by four Pratt & Whitney Wasp Major air-cooled engines gave a cruising speed of 340 mph.

A slice through the main fuselage would look like an upside-down figure eight.

Few planes have begun life in military service and ended up as luxury passenger airliners. But the Boeing 337 Stratocruiser did. During World War II, Boeing produced the "fat-bellied" Stratofreighters for use as military transports. In 1949, it produced a civilian version for Pan Am. Outside, the design of the Stratocruiser wasn't much different, but inside were sleeping berths, galleys, and a lower-deck lounge bar—a level of luxury new to civilian air travel.

Definitions
berth: Bed, usually on a train or ship.

Did You Know?

The civilian Stratocruiser and military Stratofreighter were based on the design of Boeing's B-29 Superfortress, the type that dropped atomic bombs on Hiroshima and Nagasaki.

Traveling in Style

Before World War II, few aircraft were used purely for pleasure. Air travel was simply too expensive. By the time that the Stratocruiser arrived, all this was starting to change. By the 1950s, tourism was literally "taking off," but flying was —and still is—an expensive business. To keep costs down, airline companies need planes that can carry large numbers of people. The Stratocruiser had an unusual figure-eight-shaped fuselage that gave it a big carrying capacity for the time. Fully loaded, it could hold 117 seated passengers, or 55 in berths. Rival aircraft such as the Douglas DC-7 or the Lockheed Constellation could carry almost as many passengers, but weren't anywhere near as luxurious. By the 1980s, Boeing's new 747s could carry 300 people. In 1995, the wide-bodied 777 "Jumbo Jet" added another 100 people to the passenger list. By 2006, Airbus A380 "Super Jumbos" will be capable of carrying around 555 people.

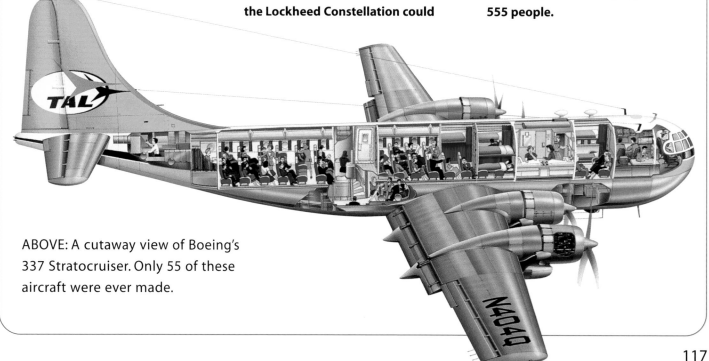

ABOVE: A cutaway view of Boeing's 337 Stratocruiser. Only 55 of these aircraft were ever made.

SAAB AJ-37 VIGGEN

Canard foreplane gives more lift to allow the plane to take off from short runways.

"Fields and Meadows" camouflage

Antiship missiles

When it was launched in the 1960s, Sweden's System 37 program was intended to produce a family of combat aircraft. What it eventually achieved was much more revolutionary. Although each version of the plane was adapted for its own specific role, all five models boasted state-of-the-art technology that made them one of the world's most advanced military aircraft. Features that have since become standard in modern tactical fighters, such as navigational computers, were first tried and tested on Saab Viggens.

Did You Know?

The word "Viggen" comes from Norse mythology. It was the name given to thunderbolts cast by the god Thor.

Thor's Hammer

ABOVE: The Viggen was built to be flexible and reliable enough to protect Sweden from aggressors.

Just in Case...

In the 1700s, Sweden was a leading power in European politics. However, for the last two hundred years the country has played no part in world conflicts. During World War II, for example, although many Swedish individuals fought against Nazi Germany, the country remained officially neutral. Despite this policy of noninvolvement, Sweden does have armed forces. In fact, it has a very large and well-equipped military, and spends around $4 billion each year on defense. The majority of troops are conscripts: All Swedish men must enlist and can be called up for a period of compulsory military service. They train and serve for around 15 months, and can be called on again in emergencies until they're 49. When the Viggen was designed, one of the requirements was that it should be easy to maintain, because up to 80 percent of the air force could be made up of untrained conscripts.

LOCKHEED AC-130H PAVE SPECTRE

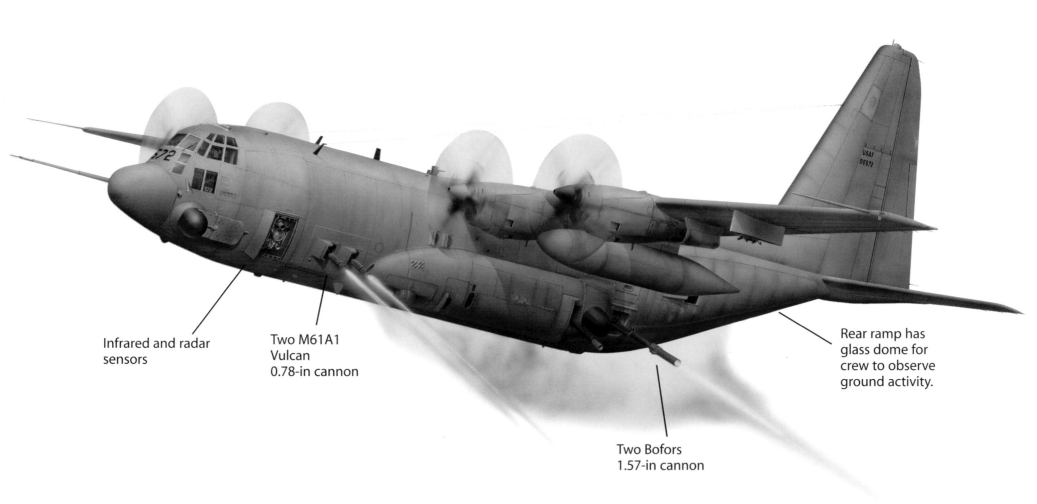

Infrared and radar sensors

Two M61A1 Vulcan 0.78-in cannon

Two Bofors 1.57-in cannon

Rear ramp has glass dome for crew to observe ground activity.

The Lockheed AC-130H, codenamed "Spectre," is an attack variant of the long-lived C-130 Hercules transport, which is in use with many air forces around the world. AC-130s were originally developed for use in the Vietnam War and successive variants have been armed with a range of more and more powerful guns. The AC-130H was adapted from the AC-130E and features better threat detection and early warning systems. Today, the "Spectre" continues to play an important role in the U.S. Air Force.

Did You Know?

Of the ten Pave Spectre 130Es made, two have been lost in combat, the first in Operation Desert Storm in the Gulf, and the second during peacekeeping work in Somalia.

How an Aircraft Gets Airborne

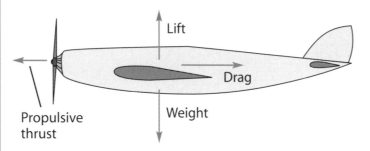

There are four main forces acting on an aircraft. The first is gravity. All things on our planet are affected by gravity, which "pulls" objects down toward the earth. Once a plane is moving, the curved top surface of the wing speeds up any air that passes over it. Under the wing, the air continues to travel at the same rate. This creates a difference in air pressure, which produces an upward force, lift. If the lift is greater than the pull of gravity, the plane will become airborne. Planes can stay up only as long as they're moving, but the forward motion of the aircraft creates drag. This means that the air surrounding the plane slows it down. To overcome this, the plane's engines need to create thrust. So, getting, and staying, airborne is a delicate balancing act!

RIGHT: Cayley's designs, such as this one for an "aerial carriage," were based on sound scientific principles, but the engines available at the time were not powerful enough.

The Father of Aviation

Sir George Cayley was born in 1773 in Scarborough, England, and is sometimes called "the father of aviation." It was Cayley who first identified the importance of gravity, lift, drag, and thrust. He also realized that the position of the wing was important—it must meet the oncoming air at an angle to create lift. This angle is now called the angle of attack, and is an important factor in the design of all modern aircraft.

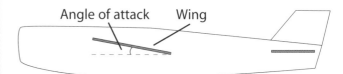

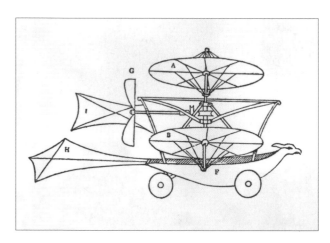

BAE/AEROSPATIALE CONCORDE

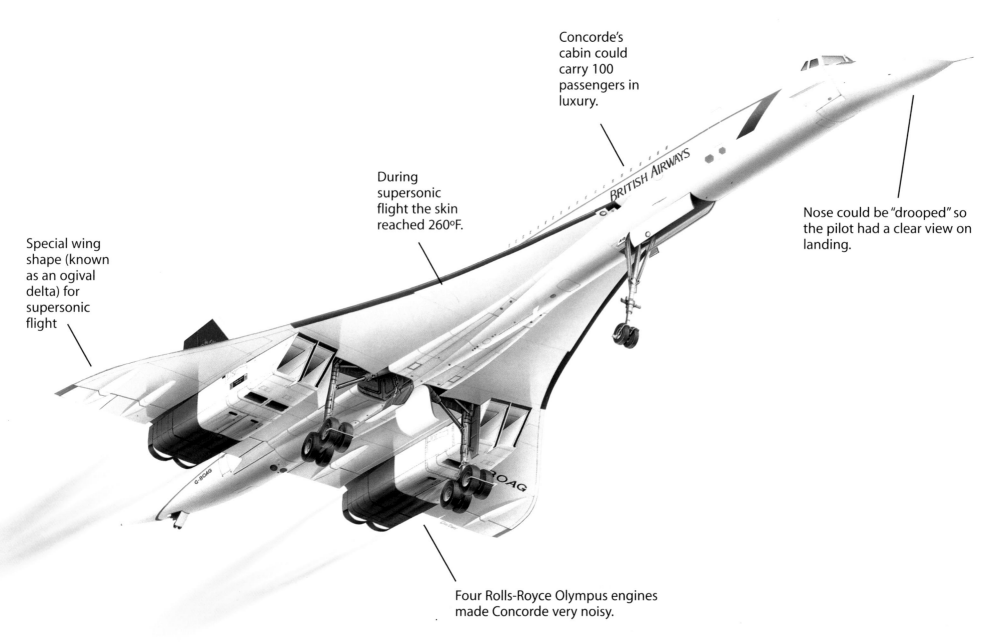

Concorde's cabin could carry 100 passengers in luxury.

During supersonic flight the skin reached 260ºF.

Nose could be "drooped" so the pilot had a clear view on landing.

Special wing shape (known as an ogival delta) for supersonic flight

Four Rolls-Royce Olympus engines made Concorde very noisy.

When British Airways (BA) retired their Concorde fleet in 2003, it signaled the end of a 27-year reign as the world's only operational supersonic passenger airliner. Built jointly by the British Aircraft Corporation and France's Aerospatiale, Concorde was one of the most technologically advanced planes ever to have been built. With space inside for just 100 passengers, it was also one of the most expensive to run and maintain. Beautiful it may have been, but it simply couldn't compete on cost with the new generation of Super Jumbos.

Faster than Sound!

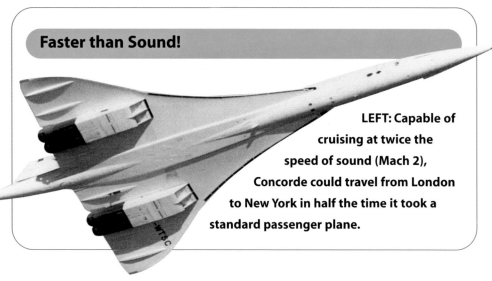

LEFT: Capable of cruising at twice the speed of sound (Mach 2), Concorde could travel from London to New York in half the time it took a standard passenger plane.

ABOVE: The Soviet competitor to Concorde, the Tupolev Tu-144, began a supersonic cargo service in 1975. Passenger services began a year later, but the aircraft was withdrawn in 1983.

Going Supersonic

In 1947, the American Bell X-1 rocket plane became the first aircraft ever to travel faster than the speed of sound. In 1953, the F-100 Super Sabre joined the supersonic record-breakers by becoming the first fighter plane to travel at such speeds. Today, planes like the SR-71 Blackbird (see pages 124–125) are capable of reaching Mach 3.5. Yet, in the 1940s, breaking what was called the "sound barrier" was considered impossible. This is because a plane traveling at very high speeds disturbs the air so much that it becomes difficult to control. In fact, if a supersonic aircraft passed overhead you would hear a loud bang, or "sonic boom," caused by disturbances or shock waves in the air created by the plane. Sonic booms are sometimes loud enough to shatter glass.

LOCKHEED SR-71 BLACKBIRD

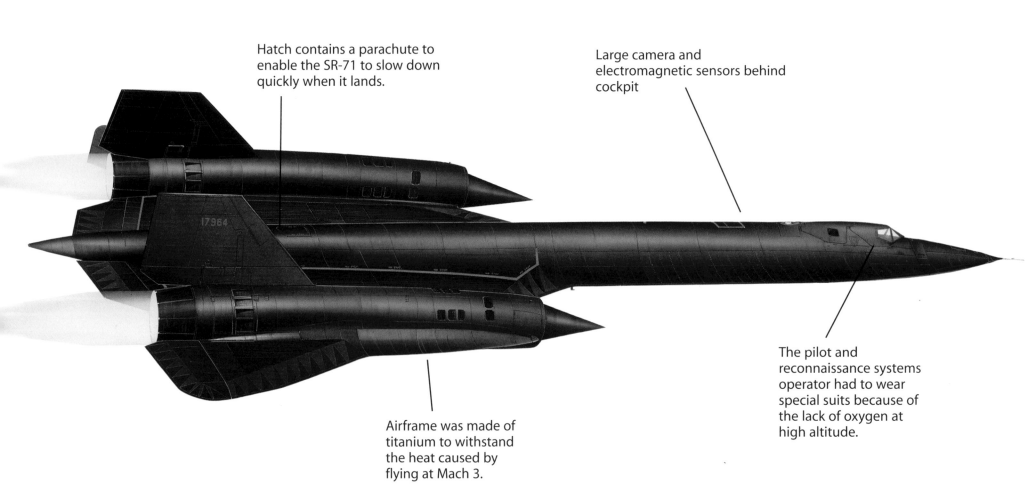

Hatch contains a parachute to enable the SR-71 to slow down quickly when it lands.

Large camera and electromagnetic sensors behind cockpit

Airframe was made of titanium to withstand the heat caused by flying at Mach 3.

The pilot and reconnaissance systems operator had to wear special suits because of the lack of oxygen at high altitude.

It's hard to believe that the first Blackbird was delivered to the U.S. Air Force in 1966—three years before Neil Armstrong walked on the moon. This futuristic-looking flying machine once held the title of the world's fastest jet, and when it was brought out of retirement in the 1990s it still outperformed its modern counterparts. Designed for high-level reconnaissance work, this "spy in the sky" is now retired again, but remains one of the true marvels of twentieth-century plane design.

Did You Know?

The SR-71 could travel so fast that friction between the air and the plane caused its outer skin to heat up to around 392°F. The black paintwork, as well as helping to disrupt enemy radar, spread the heat. At top temperatures, this paint would turn blue!

Blackbirds over Vietnam

ABOVE: Only 32 SR-71s were built. The missions they flew over Vietnam are among the fastest ever recorded.

ABOVE: The first "flight suit" was designed by Dr. Wilbur Franks in 1941 to prevent pilots passing out when subjected to high g-forces. Modern-day pilots wear a range of sophisticated protective gear.

Protective Gear

The SR-71 is capable of flying at a height of 98,000 ft. That's so high that it technically qualifies the crew as astronauts! SR-71 crews wore protective clothing, very like space suits, designed to protect them from the low pressure and lack of oxygen at that height, should anything go wrong.

Specialized clothing also helps fast jet pilots cope with g-forces. High-speed maneuvers put tremendous strain on a pilot's body. This strain—not unlike the sensation you feel when turning sharply on a roller coaster ride—is measured in "gravities," or "g." One g is equal to the normal force of Earth's gravity, and two gs is equal to twice the force of Earth's gravity. Jet pilots can pass out from the effect of high g-forces. To prevent blackouts, jet pilots wear one-piece g-suits that are automatically filled with compressed air during high-speed maneuvers, squeezing the pilot's legs and abdomen to prevent blood from rushing from his head.

LOCKHEED F-117 NIGHTHAWK

Flat panels and
angles help to reflect
radar signals.

Surface coated with
radar-absorbing
material (RAM)

Cold air is mixed with
the hot exhaust gases
to prevent the heat
from the engines being
detected.

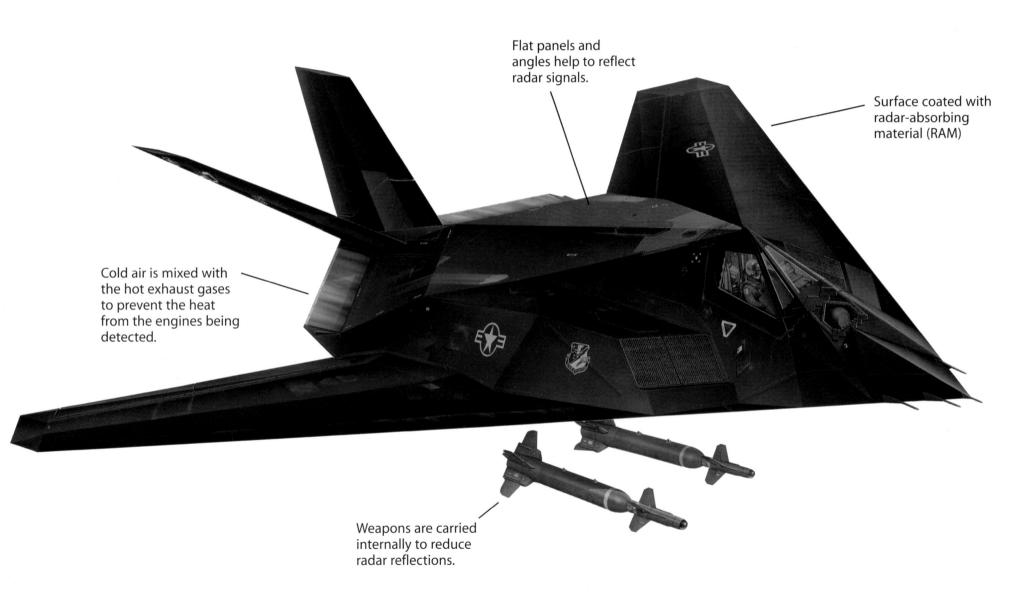

Weapons are carried
internally to reduce
radar reflections.

126

The bizarre, futuristic F-117 Nighthawk was first used in combat during the Gulf War in 1991. This "stealth" bomber was the world's first fully operational aircraft to utilize radar-evading technology. During Operation Desert Storm, this stealth technology proved to be so effective that, during more than 1,271 missions flown, not a single plane was hit by antiaircraft missiles.

How Aerofoils Work

An aerofoil is any surface designed to produce lift. On an airplane, the wing is the main aerofoil. As the plane travels through the air, the curved "leading edge" of the wing divides the air flow into two. As can be seen on the diagram, the air speeds up over the curved wing surface, but travels at the same rate below. This creates greater air pressure beneath the wing than above it, which causes lift. Turbulence is what happens when air currents are disturbed. Turbulence can make it difficult to control a plane, so it's important that, when the air flows merge at the rear of the wing, it happens smoothly.

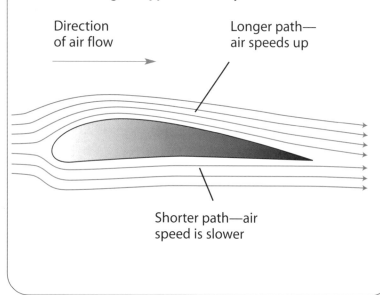

Direction of air flow

Longer path—air speeds up

Shorter path—air speed is slower

Swept wing

Delta wing

What Are Swept Wings?

When planes fly near the speed of sound, drag increases dramatically. The best way to prevent this is to give a plane a more streamlined profile (see page 13). Early planes had wings that stuck out horizontally from the fuselage, which caused drag and prevented them from breaking the sound barrier. Leaning the wings back toward the body of the plane reduces drag. This swept-back design can be seen on the F-117's wings, which are at an angle of 65 degrees. This not only helps cut drag (and so makes the plane go faster), but it also helps to reduce radar reflections. Delta wings, named after the Greek letter D, are also a popular option on fighters.

MCDONNELL DOUGLAS F-15E STRIKE EAGLE

Two-seat state-of-
the-art cockpit

Range of around
2,700 miles

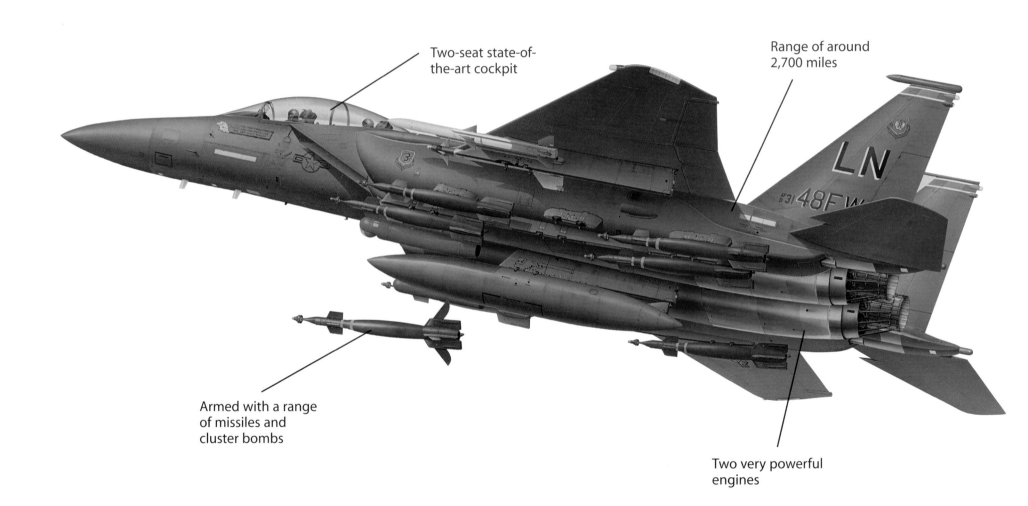

Armed with a range
of missiles and
cluster bombs

Two very powerful
engines

Since fighters like the F-117 Nighthawk cost around $45 million each, when you have a winning design it makes sense to stick with it. That's why the F-15 Eagle series has been ruling the skies since the 1972. First in the family was the F-15A, which was developed as a fighter and later adapted for ground-attack missions. The F-15C, an upgraded A, arrived in 1979. Then came the F-15D, a two-seat trainer version of the C, and finally, the star of the family, the F-15E Strike Eagle.

Did You Know?

The Strike Eagle can carry up to 24,000 pounds of armaments.

Bombs Away!

Long before the Wright Brothers made their famous 12-second flight at Kitty Hawk, military strategists understood the advantages of being able to attack their enemy from the air. To knock out an enemy base might cost the lives of thousands of soldiers, but bombs, dropped from the air, could achieve the same result with less risk to their troops. Bombs could also be used to devastate civilian towns and cities, weakening morale and destroying armament factories.

During World War II, bombers became a vital part of the war effort, supporting troops on the ground and attacking enemy targets. However, aiming was generally "by eye" and many bombs fell short or missed targets entirely. Today's bombers use computer and satellite technology to ensure that bombs are accurately dropped. Tactical bombers like the Strike Eagle also have an array of specialized weaponry, including air-to-air missiles, air-to-ground missiles, laser guided bombs, cluster bombs, and so-called "smart" missiles like the

GBU-28 pictured at left. This missile is laser-guided to enable pilots to attack specific targets like bridges without endangering large numbers of civilians. The AGM-88 HARM, right, is a High Speed Anti-Radiation Missile, used against radar installations.

GBU-28

AGM-88 HARM

BRITISH AEROSPACE HARRIER GR.5

Small air "puffers" in the nose, tail, and wingtips help stabilize the aircraft when hovering.

The Harrier's engine needs lots of air when it is hovering, so the intake is larger than on other jets.

This is a Royal Air Force Harrier based at RAF Wittering.

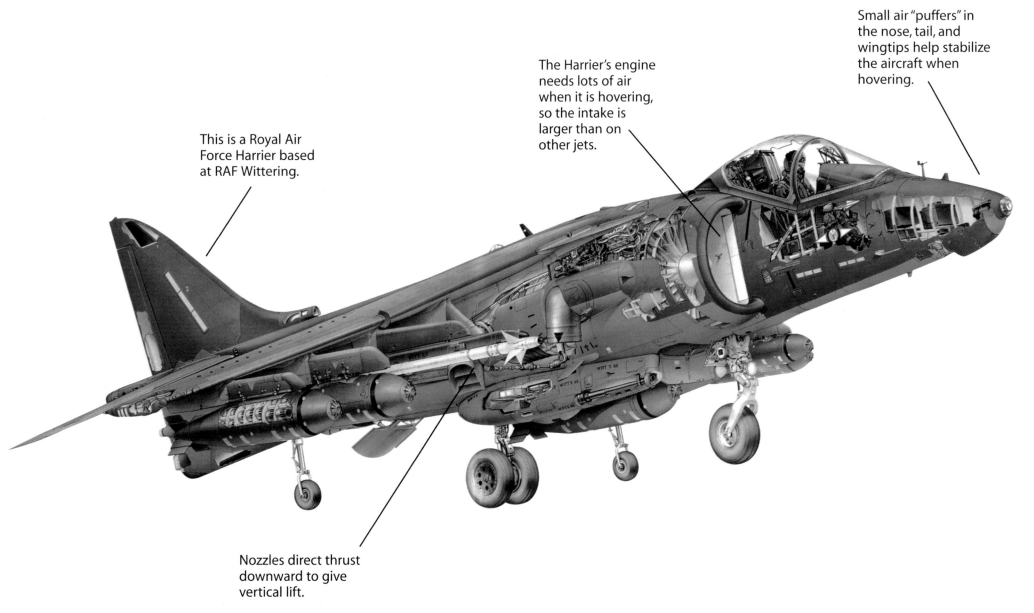

Nozzles direct thrust downward to give vertical lift.

The dream of many military aircraft designers has always been a plane that could take off and land vertically. Not only would this do away with the need for large, expensive aircraft carriers, but it would also enable fighters to operate from bases near the front line in a war. The remarkable Harrier was the first ever vertical takeoff and landing (VTOL) aircraft to enter service, and has proved itself a formidable opponent in battle.

Did You Know?

The Harrier is named after a bird of prey that hovers before it attacks.

Battle Tested

When Argentina invaded the British Falkland Islands in 1982, Harriers were still untested in battle. Although its VTOL technology was impressive, there was real concern that the plane would be outgunned and out-maneuvered by the Argentinian Air Force's faster Mirages and Skyhawks. Because the islands were so remote, British forces had to operate from aircraft carriers, but the British Navy had so few Sea Harriers that the RAF's land-based GR.3 Harriers had to be adapted. Within days of arriving in the Falklands, however, the Harrier proved to be more than a match for the opposition. The plane turned out to be not just a vertical takeoff specialist but an extremely flexible combat aircraft. During the hostilities, Harriers showed that they could fly equally well whether at 250 or 40,000 feet. In dogfights they were said to be so effective that the Argentinians nicknamed them "the black death."

The Flying Bedstead

This early design for a Vertical Take Off and Landing (VTOL) plane, built by Rolls-Royce in 1953, was called the flying bedstead for obvious reasons! Rolls-Royce later joined with aircraft manufacturer Hawker Siddeley (later part of British Aerospace) to make the Harrier, developing the pioneering Rolls-Royce Pegasus engine that powers the aircraft. The Harrier has nozzles attached to the engine, to direct the thrust downward. When hovering, air "puffers" on each corner of the plane keep it stable.

NORTHROP GRUMMAN B-2A SPIRIT

The unique shape is
designed to deflect radar.

Four General Electric F118-GE-100
turbofan engines are buried deep within
the aircraft.

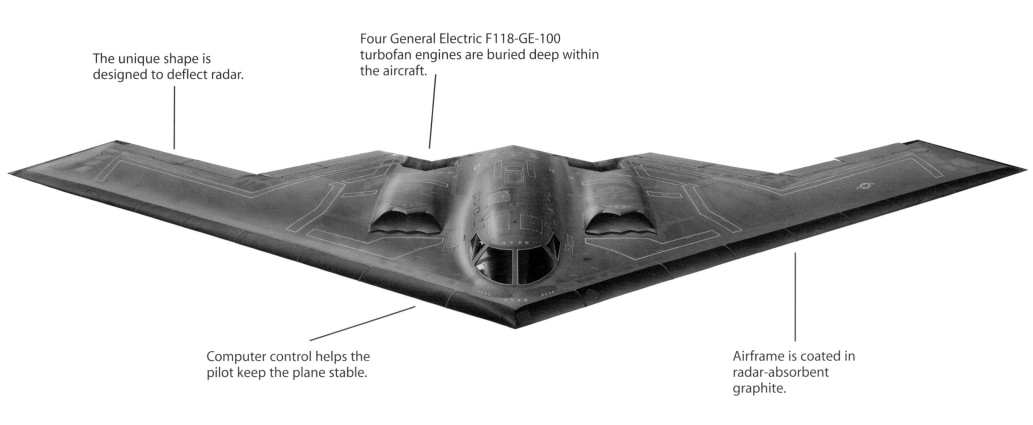

Computer control helps the
pilot keep the plane stable.

Airframe is coated in
radar-absorbent
graphite.

Jack Northrop was probably one of the twentieth century's most innovative aircraft designers. Although he worked for both Lockheed and Douglas, it's his name that is carried by the futuristic-looking B-2A Spirit. Produced at the height of the Cold War, and playing a key role in the U.S. Air Force's strike capability today, this stealth bomber is not only virtually invisible to radar but can hit any target in the world from its base inside the United States.

Did You Know?

Just one B-2A Spirit costs around $2 billion, which is why just 20 of these remarkable planes were built.

Northrop Flying Wing Designs

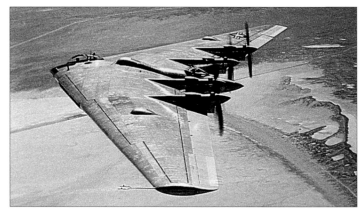

ABOVE: Northrop gained a great deal of experience building flying wing designs; this is the XB-35, which flew in the 1940s.

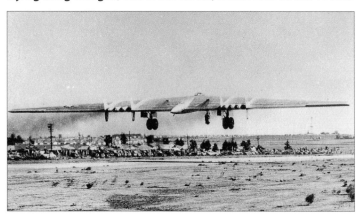

ABOVE: This is the Northrop YB-49, a jet-engined bomber design that flew in 1947, 40 years before the B-2A.

What Is a Flying Wing?

With no fuselage and no tail, the B-2A seems to defy all the laws of aerodynamics. In fact, it's not really a regular plane, it's a flying wing. The idea behind this revolutionary design seems simple. It's the wing that gives the plane lift. All other parts slow the aircraft down and create drag. So, in theory, if a plane could be all wing it would be faster than other planes, and more fuel efficient. A flying wing design, with fewer angles and mainly straight lines, would also be very "stealthy" (see pages 126–127). Unfortunately, without a traditional tail, planes lack stability. Also, the pilot, instrumentation, fuel, and engines have to be squeezed into the wing shape. Northrop struggled with these problems before inventing the first true flying wing, the N-1M, in 1940. The XB-35 followed in 1946. This huge bomber could carry over five tons of bombs, at 391 mph. Compare this to the B-17 Flying Fortress, which could carry less than one ton of bombs at a top speed of 287 mph, and it's clear that the XB-35 was truly ground-breaking. Northrop's crowning achievement, though, was to come 40 years later with the B-2. With just a few bulges on the wing's surface for crew, bombs, and engines, this plane is pure design brilliance.

CHAPTER SEVEN

Helicopters

*They've been called whirlybirds, eggbeaters, and windys,
and there's no doubt that helicopters look strange enough
to deserve all of these names.*

With wide, fat bodies, and huge rotating blades on top, helicopters seem like the oddest of flying machines. Yet, they can do things that most planes can't. They can take off and land without the need for an airstrip. They can fly straight up or down, backward or forward. They can even hover with ease. These amazing abilities have made helicopters one of the modern world's most widely used and flexible vehicles. From small taxi helicopters to heavy-duty cargo carriers and armored military troop transports, the helicopter may be an odd-looking bird, but it's certainly a useful one!

BELL AH-1 HUEYCOBRA

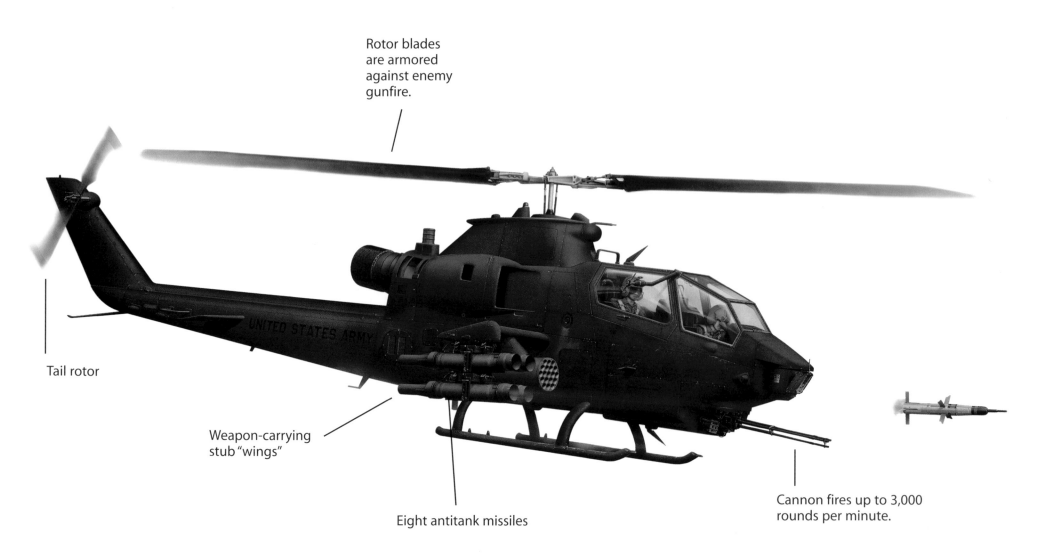

Rotor blades
are armored
against enemy
gunfire.

Tail rotor

Weapon-carrying
stub "wings"

Eight antitank missiles

Cannon fires up to 3,000
rounds per minute.

If ever an aircraft or helicopter could strike fear into the heart of an enemy just by its menacing appearance, it has to be the AH-1 HueyCobra. Developed from the famous UH-1 Huey, pictured at right, the AH-1 was specially designed to support ground troops and was heavily armed. The first HueyCobra flew in 1965 and the type saw combat in Vietnam just two years later.

Did You Know?

The HueyCobra is fitted with wire cutters above and below the cockpit, in case it flies into power cables when operating at low altitude.

The Huey and the "Air-Cav"

Thanks to movies like *Apocalypse Now,* the Vietnam War is now firmly identified with helicopters like the AH-1 HueyCobra and its predecessor, the UH-1 Huey (pictured above). However, when the Huey first arrived in Vietnam, the idea of using helicopters in a war zone was new. The thick jungles of the region made it impossible for planes to land, which called for a new type of warfare, known as "air mobility." This relied on helicopters like the UH-1 Huey, which were adapted to do a variety of jobs. Hueys were used for reconnaissance, as troop carriers, to ferry wounded from the battlefield, and—with the addition of two 1.18-inch machine guns and two 2.75-inch rocket launchers — as "gunships" to give covering fire to men on the ground. Because the Hueys had been so successful in this role, a more specialized attack helicopter, the AH-1 HueyCobra, was developed. Aboard these helicopters were members of a new formation, the First Cavalry Division (known as the Air-Cav), whose roots went back to the days of the horse cavalry in the early twentieth century. In fact, the commander of the First Cavalry Division, Colonel John Stockton, took the division's cavalry heritage so seriously that he ordered black cowboy hats for all his men, and had his officers wear handlebar mustaches like those worn in the past.

BOEING CHINOOK

Two main rotors (known as a tandem-rotor design) give extra lift.

This illustration shows an RAF Chinook HC. 1. Chinooks were British RAF during the Falklands conflict in 1982.

ROYAL AIR FORCE

ZA718

EQ

Rear door for rapid loading and unloading

Nonretractable sturdy undercarriage

Frank Piasecki was one of the pioneers of tandem-rotor helicopters, so, when Piasecki's company, Vertol (standing for Vertical Take-Off and Landing), was taken over by Boeing in 1960, it wasn't too surprising that Boeing-Vertol's next project should be a tandem-rotor machine. The Chinook was designed specifically for the U.S. Army. With two massive rotors to keep it airborne, this powerful workhorse has become the military's very own "flying truck."

Forty Years of Hard Work

ABOVE: The Chinook has been in service, with modifications and upgrades, since the 1960s. This example is being used to fight forest fires in Spain.

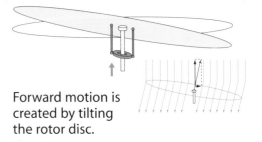

Changing the angle of attack (or pitch) increases lift.

Forward motion is created by tilting the rotor disc.

Did You Know?

The Chinook has been nicknamed "big windy" because of the amount of air that is stirred up by its huge rotors.

How Helicopters Fly

A helicopter's rotor blades are, in effect, huge movable wings. The shape of the rotor is curved on the upper surface and flat on the lower. As the rotor moves through the air, the air traveling over the blades moves faster than the air below, creating a difference in air pressure. This generates lift. Pilots can adjust the amount of lift by adjusting the angle of the blades against the air. This is called the "angle of attack" and is the same principle as used in airplane design. The blades on a helicopter can be collectively tilted to give a greater angle of attack. However, by increasing this "collective pitch," more air is pulled through the blades. Air creates drag as well as lift, so when the angle of attack is increased, the power going to the blades from the engine must also be increased. If it wasn't, drag would slow the blades down and the helicopter wouldn't be able to stay in the air. When the rotor disc is tilted, as shown above, the air is directed backward, pushing the helicopter forward.

WESTLAND LYNX

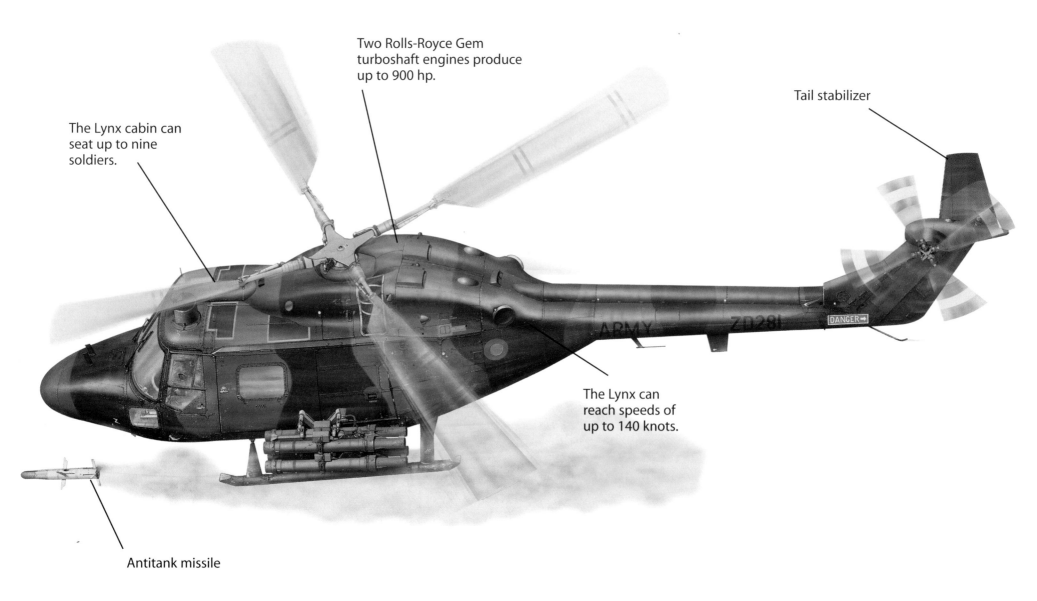

Two Rolls-Royce Gem turboshaft engines produce up to 900 hp.

Tail stabilizer

The Lynx cabin can seat up to nine soldiers.

The Lynx can reach speeds of up to 140 knots.

Antitank missile

The Westland Lynx was initially produced for the British Army Air Corps. These fast and flexible helicopters have since been used for everything from reconnaissance to the evacuation of casualties, troop transport, and armed escorts. Fitted with up to eight missiles, the Lynx also makes an extremely effective tank buster. Royal Marine versions, such as the Lynx HAS Mk.3, have been adapted for a similar role at sea; the addition of depth charges, torpedoes, or Sea Skua missiles make them deadly in antisubmarine warfare.

What Is Torque?

Like all aircraft, helicopters are subject to the forces of gravity, lift, drag, and thrust (see page 121). However, because helicopters have a rotating wing (the rotor), they are also subject to another force: torque. Torque is caused by any twisting movement. When the rotor on a helicopter turns, torque will cause the fuselage to twist around in the opposite direction. So, to stop the body of the helicopter spinning out of control, single-rotor helicopters don't have one rotor, but at least two! The second is a tail rotor, which does not create enough thrust to lift the helicopter, but does help keep it straight. It does this by pushing the tail of the helicopter against the force of torque. If power is increased to the main rotor, it must also be increased by the same amount to the tail rotor. In tandem-rotor helicopters, such as the Chinook, there's no need for a tail rotor. The helicopter's two main rotors simply turn in opposite directions, which cancels out torque.

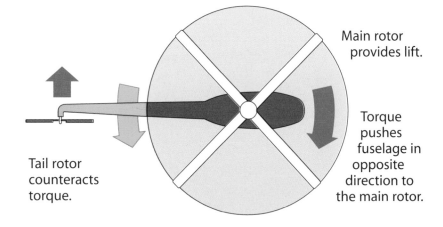

Main rotor provides lift.

Tail rotor counteracts torque.

Torque pushes fuselage in opposite direction to the main rotor.

ABOVE: The Cierva W.9 did not have a second rotor to cancel out the torque. This experimental helicopter used a jet instead of a tail rotor to control its stability.

Definitions

knot: A measurement of speed used by naval vessels and aircraft. One knot is 1.15 land miles.

Did You Know?

Military vehicles have model numbers that tell us what they were designed for. For example, the Sikorsky CH series are "Cargo Helicopters." Apache AH models are Attack Helicopters.

SIKORSKY SH-60 SEAHAWK

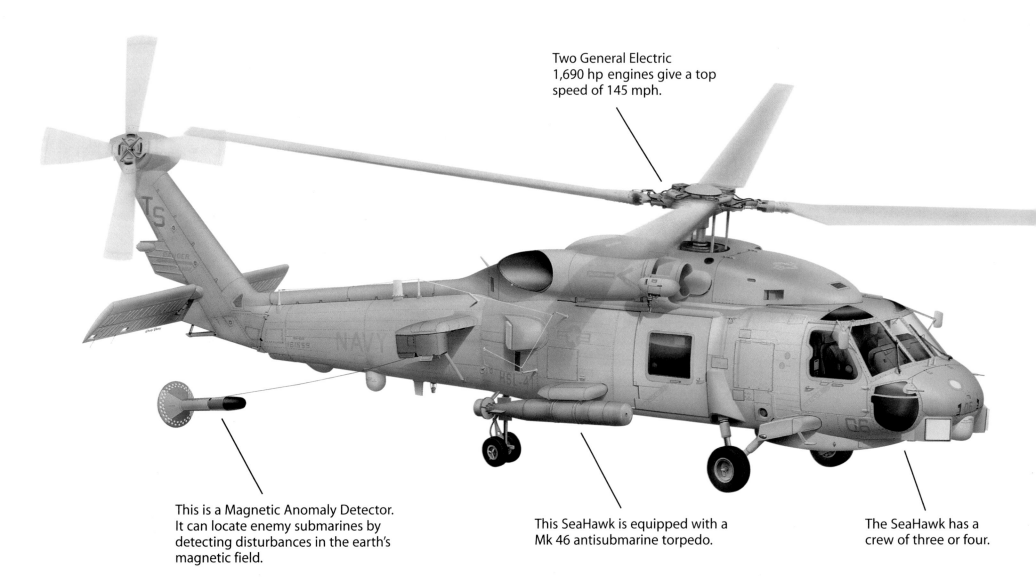

Two General Electric 1,690 hp engines give a top speed of 145 mph.

This is a Magnetic Anomaly Detector. It can locate enemy submarines by detecting disturbances in the earth's magnetic field.

This SeaHawk is equipped with a Mk 46 antisubmarine torpedo.

The SeaHawk has a crew of three or four.

Over the last 80 years, Sikorsky's name has come to be one of the most trusted and admired in helicopter design, and its helicopters have been used by the military since World War II. The powerful H-60 series is in service with the U.S. Army, the U.S. Air Force, and the U.S. Navy. The SH-60B model shown here is a "sub-hunter" and is equipped with an array of sophisticated submarine-detecting equipment, as well as deadly torpedoes.

Definitions
mechanics: The study of motion and forces.

Did You Know?

Military helicopters are expensive. A single Black Hawk, for example, costs around $6 million.

Leonardo da Vinci's Helicopter Design

ABOVE: Leonardo's helicopter was a huge screwlike device, 13 feet in diameter. It was to be propelled by four men running around the central shaft, to turn the spiral and create lift. However, Leonardo forgot about torque.

Designs for the Future

Many people know Leonardo as the great Italian painter who gave the world the *Mona Lisa*. Yet he was as interested in science as in art. His particular passion was for the science of mechanics, and much of his later life was spent designing moving machines. In his birthplace—Vinci, near Florence—a museum dedicated to the town's most famous son has produced models based on a few of these remarkable designs. This includes an "auto-mobile," doodled by Leonardo 431 years before Ford's Model T rolled off the production lines. Leonardo's auto is nothing like a modern car, being made from wood and propelled by huge springs. Yet many of his other sketches seem more familiar, and include a tank, a submarine, and even a helicopter. Most of his ideas never got past the drawing-board stage, and many would probably never work. But Leonardo's ingenuity and creativity has inspired inventors and scientists for centuries.

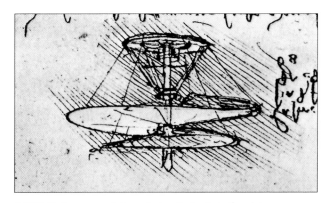

ABOVE: Leonardo's original sketch for his helicopter design.

SIKORSKY CH-53D SEA STALLION

The six huge blades are made of aluminum and can be folded when the machine is parked.

This pipe allows the helicopter to refuel in midair from a tanker. It has to be very long to keep the rotor out of the way of the tanker aircraft.

Rear loading doors and ramp speed up loading and unloading.

Larger loads can be carried in slings hung below the helicopter.

When it was developed, the CH-53D Sea Stallion was the largest Sikorsky helicopter ever. Designed for cargo and troop transport, this 88-foot-long beast has an impressive carrying capacity. With rear-loading doors, and on-board winches, the CH-53D is capable of transporting a 1.5-ton truck over 257 miles. As a troop transport, it can deliver 38 fully equipped troops to their destination at a top speed of 196 mph.

Did You Know?

Air Force versions of the CH-53 were used for search and rescue work in Vietnam, where they earned the nickname "Jolly Green Giants."

The Sikorsky Story

When Igor Sikorsky arrived in America from Russia in 1919, his dream was to pursue a career in aircraft design. Sikorsky had trained as an engineer and had achieved great success with a series of airplane designs, including the world's first four-engined aircraft. However, after the Russian Revolution, Sikorsky became convinced that Communist Russia wouldn't be able to offer him the opportunities that he would have elsewhere, so he traveled to the United States to look for work. After a few years, however, he was forced to start teaching to pay the bills. At first, Sikorsky lectured in mathematics, but soon his natural passion for aeronautics started to filter into his lectures. Astronomy and aviation were soon added to the list of topics that he taught. It was this which gave Sikorsky his first big break. Aviation enthusiasts flocked to his talks and encouraged him to set up his own company to design and build aircraft for himself. Sikorsky's company was founded in 1923 and soon his designs were breaking records for speed and performance. By the 1930s, his range of flying boats had made him both rich and famous. Yet Sikorsky's real passion was for helicopters, and in 1939 he produced the world's first workable single-rotor helicopter, shown here. Today, the Sikorsky Company continues to make cutting-edge, world-beating helicopters.

MIL MI-24 "HIND-D"

Main rotor has five blades (two to eight is standard for a single-rotor helicopter).

Four-barrel turret-mounted machine gun

2.24-inch rockets

Tail bumper prevents the tail rotor from hitting the ground.

One look at the Russian Mil Mi-24 will tell you that it shares many features with American attack helicopters like the AH-1 HueyCobra or AH-64 Apache. All have short, stubby, weapon-carrying "wings," lots of bulletproof windows for all-around vision, and a powerful cannon under the fuselage. Code-named "Hind" during the Cold War by the West, the Mi-24 is a formidable combat helicopter, and can also be used for troop transport —it has space for up to eight soldiers inside.

Did You Know?

The Mi-24 was used extensively during Russia's war in Afghanistan, and is now used by at least 34 countries worldwide.

How Does the Pilot Control a Helicopter?

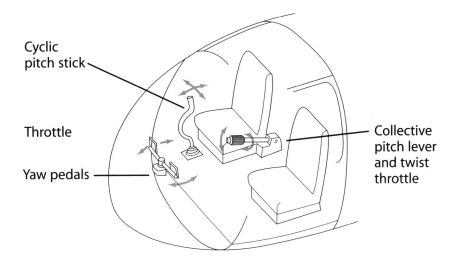

Cyclic pitch stick

Throttle

Yaw pedals

Collective pitch lever and twist throttle

This illustration shows the basic controls in a helicopter cockpit. Designs differ, but in most helicopters there are four main controls that pilots must learn to control before they can fly the machine:

1. **The "yaw," or rudder, pedals control the angle (or pitch) of the tail rotor. To turn left or right, the pilot presses either the left or right pedal.**
2. **The cyclic pitch stick or control column. This is moved in the appropriate direction to give backward, forward, or sideways flight.**
3. **The collective pitch lever. This changes the rotor's angle of attack. By making fine adjustments to the pitch lever, the helicopter can climb, hover, or descend.**
4. **The throttle is used to increase or decrease engine power.**

Years of Training

Learning to use these pedals and levers is a very complex and time-consuming process. It can take many years to master properly, and has been compared to patting your head and rubbing your stomach at the same time. Try it! Military helicopters are even more difficult to handle, with guns and missiles, aiming systems, sensors, and early-warning devices added to the mix. Helicopters like the Mi-24 actually have two pilots, who work in tandem cockpits.

ABOVE: A Mil Mi-24 "Hind" in action. More than 2,500 of these helicopters have been sold around the world.

BOEING AH-64D LONGBOW APACHE

Longbow mast-
mounted radar

Four-blade "articulated"
(in sections) rotor

Night vision, laser tracker,
and television screen to
aid targeting

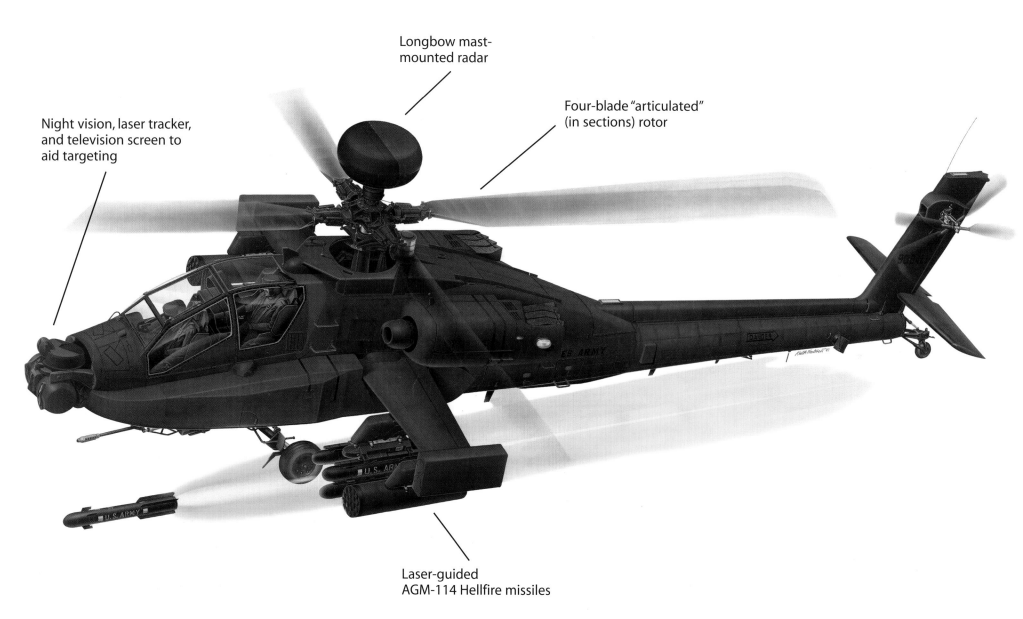

Laser-guided
AGM-114 Hellfire missiles

When it was delivered to the U.S. military in 1982, the AH-64A Apache was probably the most lethal attack helicopter in the world. The upgraded AH-64D, which arrived in 1997, is considered to be four times as effective. Designed to fight and survive, day or night, in any weather conditions, the Longbow Apache is equipped with state-of-the-art technology that enables it to find, identify, and attack potential enemy targets within an incredible 30 seconds.

Did You Know?

Longbow Apaches have taken part in major conflicts in the Gulf, as well as peacekeeping operations in Bosnia and Kosovo.

Civilian Helicopters

It's a fact that during times of war, technology makes huge leaps forward. In 1903, the Wrights had only just made their first engine-powered flight in a flimsy wooden biplane. By 1915, the first all-metal single-winged plane had been built. By 1930, Frank Whittle had already invented the jet engine. If it wasn't for the two World Wars, much of this technology would have never left the drawing board. Military need—and cash—pushes science forward. Whether we're talking about trucks, planes, or helicopters, military examples tend to be the most technologically advanced, and the benefits are felt

Keeping the Peace

ABOVE: Helicopters are valued by police forces worldwide for their ability to hover for long periods of time.

ABOVE: A Westland Sea King helicopter practicing a rescue at sea.

in the civilian world. For example, in the construction industry, helicopters are invaluable for those hard-to-reach jobs, such as installing air-conditioning units on the top of skyscrapers. In agriculture, small lightweight helicopters can spray crops more accurately than traditional crop sprayers. Where the helicopter has really proved its worth, though, is in emergency work, especially in areas that planes or vehicles can't reach. For mountain rescue, air-sea rescue, fire services, and air-ambulance teams, the helicopter has become a true lifesaver.

GEE

GEEST ST LUCIA

CHAPTER EIGHT

Ships and Submarines

Ships are one of the oldest forms of transportation. Since ancient times, people have hollowed out logs or made rafts from reeds in an attempt to cross the seas and oceans.

At first, perhaps, people were driven by a desire to explore and learn more about the world around them. Later, as technology improved, ships were used to transport people, goods, and even armies around the world. Almost as soon as humankind discovered that the earth was a globe, sailors strived to circumnavigate the planet, driven by the desire to find new trade routes and foreign treasures. Soon ships were allowing vast numbers of people to travel the world, for business and for pleasure. From sailing ships to steam-powered vessels, and from tankers to luxury liners and submarines, our love affair with the sea has continued to this day.

CUTTY SARK TEA CLIPPER

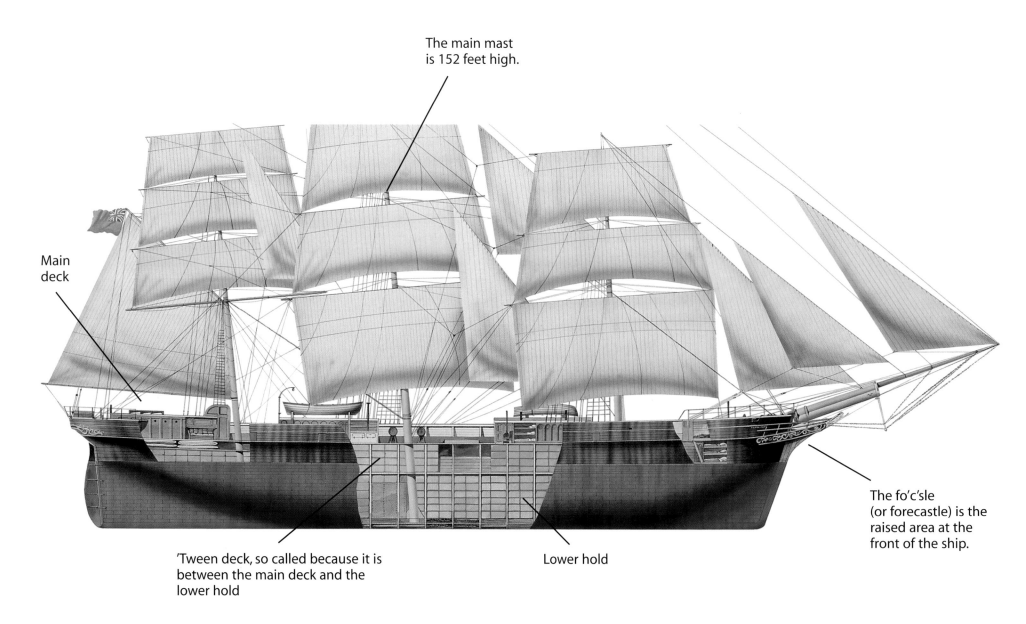

The main mast is 152 feet high.

Main deck

'Tween deck, so called because it is between the main deck and the lower hold

Lower hold

The fo'c'sle (or forecastle) is the raised area at the front of the ship.

In the nineteenth century, fast, slender sailing ships were known as clippers. When she set sail in 1870, the *Cutty Sark* was one of the world's fastest clippers. Part of the reason for this was the *Cutty Sark's* beautiful, sleek hull design. The other was the large amount of sail that she carried. Fully rigged, the *Cutty Sark* had 43 sails. This was the nineteenth-century equivalent of putting in a turbocharged engine—and it enabled this beautiful little ship to cut though the ocean waves at up to 14 knots.

Did You Know?

Clippers were developed in America in the 1800s. They were given their name because of the way they "clipped" through the miles.

Ocean-Going Express

ABOVE: During her time in the wool trade, the *Cutty Sark* continually set records for the fastest journey between Australia and England.

Born to Race

The *Cutty Sark* was built at the request of John "White Hat" Willis. For ship owners like Willis, speed was the key to business success. Whoever had the fastest ships could bring their cargoes home first and get the highest prices. At the time, the fastest ship on the tea route from China to England was the *Thermopylae*. Willis determined that his new ship would be sleeker, stronger, and faster than any on the sea. Unfortunately, although the *Cutty Sark* was to set many records during her later career, she never beat the *Thermopylae*. In fact, in the same year she was built, the Suez Canal opened and, as sailing ships couldn't travel through the canal, clippers started to fall out of favor. By the 1890s, the *Cutty Sark* had been sold and she spent the next 30 years laboring as a general cargo carrier. This ended in 1922, when she was spotted by Captain Wilfred Dowman, who remembered the beautiful little clipper at the height of her fame and determined to restore her to her former glory. Today, she is in dry dock in Greenwich, London, but the annual Tall Ships Race is a reminder of how graceful sailing ships like the *Cutty Sark* can be.

R.M.S. *TITANIC* OCEAN LINER

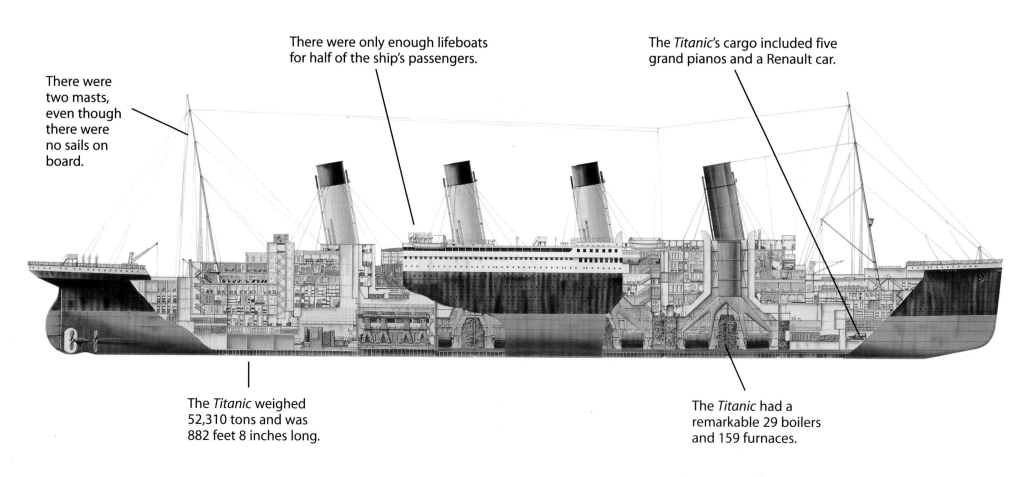

There were only enough lifeboats for half of the ship's passengers.

The *Titanic*'s cargo included five grand pianos and a Renault car.

There were two masts, even though there were no sails on board.

The *Titanic* weighed 52,310 tons and was 882 feet 8 inches long.

The *Titanic* had a remarkable 29 boilers and 159 furnaces.

Few ships are as famous as the *Titanic*. When she set out on her maiden (first) voyage in 1912, she was the biggest and most spectacular passenger liner of her time. Yet, the *Titanic's* fame has nothing to do with her size or the luxury of her design. It's her sinking, in the ice-bound waters of the North Atlantic Ocean, and the tragic loss of life that continues to fascinate and enthrall.

· ·

Definitions
hull: Body of the ship.
beam: Ship's widest point.

· ·

Did You Know?

The captain of the *Titanic*, Captain Edward J. Smith, went down with his ship. After a 25-year career, which he described as "uneventful," he intended to retire after the voyage.

Ghostly Wreck at the Bottom of the Atlantic

ABOVE: Dr. Robert Ballard discovered the wreck of the *Titanic* in 1985.

The Story of the *Titanic*

Few of the 2,209 who boarded the *Titanic* at Southampton on April 10, 1912, would have imagined that, within five days, the ship and all but 705 passengers would be lost beneath the ocean. The *Titanic* was the pride of the White Star Line, and was popularly believed to be unsinkable. The ship's hull was divided into 16 airtight compartments. In a disaster, the ship would still float with two of these compartments entirely flooded. When the ship collided with an iceberg, however, six of these compartments were flooded, and the "unsinkable" *Titanic* was sucked beneath the waves in just under two and a half hours. The story is tragic, but why should we remember the *Titanic* more than any other ship? Aboard were playboy millionaires, statesmen, diplomats, and thousands of poor families hoping to start a new life in America. It's these individual experiences that make the *Titanic's* story so moving. How could we forget stories such as that of Mrs. Ida Straus, wife of the owner of Macy's stores, who calmly refused a seat on a lifeboat and chose instead to die beside her husband? Even if Dr. Ballard hadn't discovered the wreck's remains in 1985, these remarkable tales of bravery would have kept the *Titanic's* story alive.

DKM *BISMARCK* BATTLESHIP

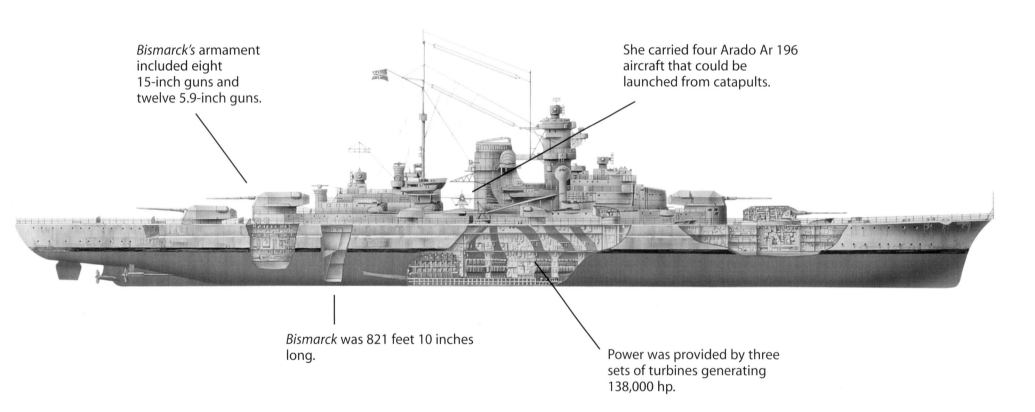

Bismarck's armament included eight 15-inch guns and twelve 5.9-inch guns.

She carried four Arado Ar 196 aircraft that could be launched from catapults.

Bismarck was 821 feet 10 inches long.

Power was provided by three sets of turbines generating 138,000 hp.

The final days of the *Bismarck* have become almost as famous as the ship itself. Launched at the height of World War II, the *Bismarck* was one of the biggest battleships of her day, and so dangerous that, from the moment she left port in February 1941, she was shadowed by ships from the British Royal Navy. When she was finally caught, after a three-month chase, a furious 88-minute battle followed, during which the *Bismarck* was hit by more than 300 shells before sinking.

Did You Know?

The wreck of the *Bismarck* was discovered in 1989 by Dr. Robert Ballard, who also found the wreck of the *Titanic* (see pages 154–155).

Bring on the Big Guns!

If modern aircraft carriers are just floating runways, then battleships were waterborne gun platforms. On board the *Bismarck,* for example, were eight vast 15-inch guns. These were adapted from coastal defense weapons and had a huge range and loading capacity. Just one armor-piercing shell from one of these guns weighed 1,765 pounds. And three of these shells could be fired accurately every minute over a distance of 45,600 yards. The reason for such raw firepower was simple. The *Bismarck* was a hunter, designed to sink ships, and her main prey was the merchant vessels that kept Britain supplied with food and vital raw materials during the war. Up against other warships, though, the *Bismarck* was just as deadly. During her long chase with the British navy, the *Bismarck* sank the cruiser *Hood* and crippled the battleship *Prince of Wales.* Yet, in terms of firepower, the *Bismarck* was not the most powerful battleship on the seas at the time. That honor went to a ship of the Japanese navy: With 18-inch guns, the Japanese *Yamato,* above, was the most heavily armed battleship ever built.

U.S.S. *NIMITZ* AIRCRAFT CARRIER

The *Nimitz* carries around 70 aircraft.

The "island" contains command and navigation bridges.

Flight deck area is 4.5 acres.

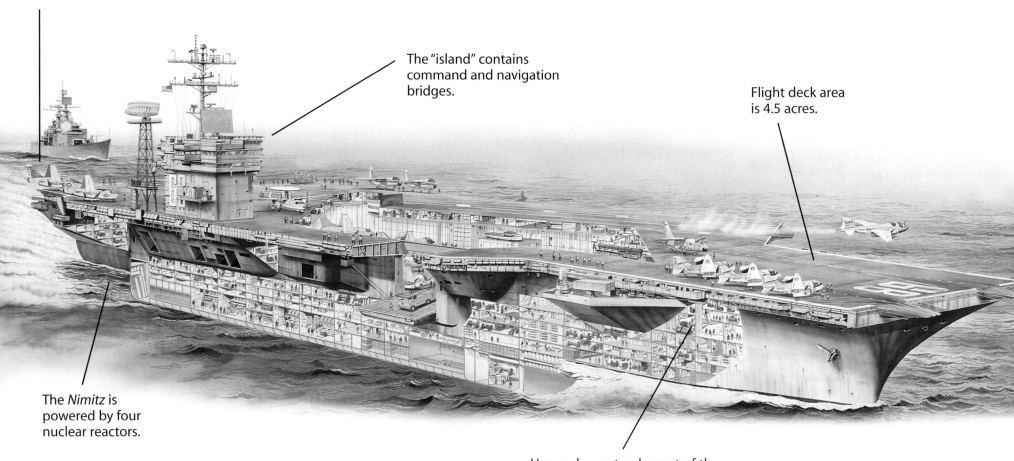

The *Nimitz* is powered by four nuclear reactors.

Hangar bay extends most of the ship's length and is used to store and maintain aircraft.

At nearly 1,092 feet long and 18 stories high, the U.S.S. *Nimitz* is an incredible sight. This "floating city" has accommodations for 6,000 people, its own 53-bed hospital, a chapel, a post office, and five dentists! At the heart of the carrier is the naval "air wing," which consists of up to 70 aircraft, from helicopters to fighters, depending on the mission. No wonder, then, that President Ford, speaking at her launch in 1975, described her as "a solid symbol of the United States' strength."

Did You Know?

The only ships larger than modern aircraft carriers are oil tankers.

A Floating Airstrip

In the past, naval battles were all about firepower. To rule the waves, battleships needed to be equipped with large, long-range guns (see pages 156–157). Today, firepower is still just as important, but most carriers need only antiaircraft guns and missiles for self-protection. Their real power lies in their aircraft. Early aircraft carriers like the U.S.S. *Langley*, which was a converted coal ship, weren't specifically made to carry planes, but modern carriers are designed as huge floating airstrips. The *Nimitz,* for example, has 4.5 acres of flight deck, and a massive hangar bay below, with space for up to 70 aircraft. Cranes are used to move aircraft around. For conventional aircraft, taking off from and landing on an aircraft carrier—even a large one like the *Nimitz*—can be difficult, so catapults are used to help them get airborne. When landing, cables stretched across a section of the deck "catch" the planes before they overshoot! Vertical takeoff and landing aircraft like Harriers are especially useful, and are used by many air forces worldwide, as are helicopters.

NORTHWEST SANDERLING TANKER

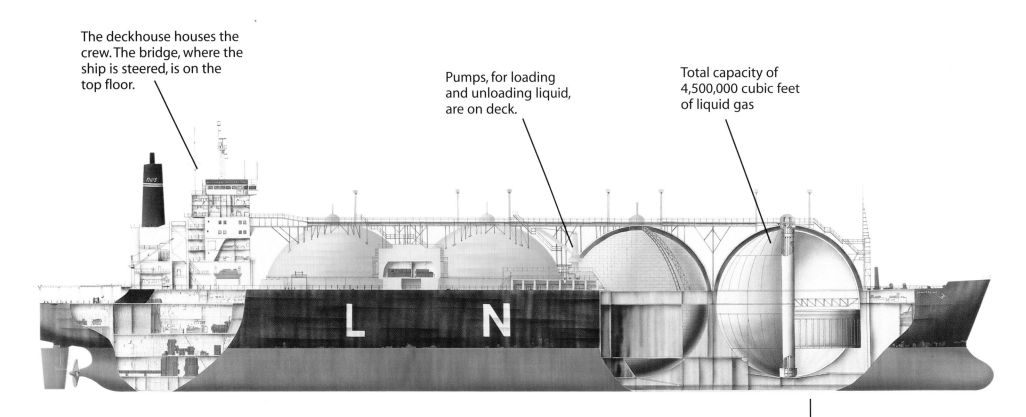

The deckhouse houses the crew. The bridge, where the ship is steered, is on the top floor.

Pumps, for loading and unloading liquid, are on deck.

Total capacity of 4,500,000 cubic feet of liquid gas

The Northwest Sanderling is 892 feet long.

Tankers are the long-distance haulage trucks of the oceans. Most tankers transport petroleum, but there's more to the *Northwest Sanderling* than meets the eye. Inside her specially designed hull is natural gas. Cooling natural gas to -261°F turns it into a liquid, so the *Northwest Sanderling* is an LNG (Liquid Natural Gas) carrier. Once the tanker arrives at its destination, the gas is returned to its natural state and pumped into our homes.

What Happens When Disaster Strikes?

The *Northwest Sanderling* carries natural gas, but most tankers carry oil. In the past, oil was transported in barrels, but it was soon realized that a ship's hull is really a large, empty barrel, so oil could be pumped straight into the hold. This saved time and money. Later, designers divided the hull into big separate tanks (eight is usual) to make the cargo more stable. Today's supertankers can carry around 440,000 tons of oil each and much of the world relies on them to deliver vital fuel cheaply and efficiently. The problem is when

Tanker Disaster!

ABOVE: The oil tanker *Erika* spilled more than 2.5 million gallons of oil into the ocean off Brittany, France, in 1999.

tankers leak: The oil can seep out into the oceans. Many modern tankers have double hulls to prevent this, but if a tanker sinks then even this precaution won't stop an oil spill. Oil spills can be disastrous for the environment. Oil forms a thick film on the surface of water, choking anything below. If the oil washes up on shore, it can poison the land and animals. Scientists are working on ways to clean up spills, but it's believed that there's no real solution. For example, when the *Exxon Valdez* tanker ran aground in Alaska in 1989, enough oil to fill 125 Olympic-size swimming pools was spilled. More than 15 years later, wildlife is still suffering the aftereffects: 250,000 birds, almost 3,000 otters, and more than 20 whales have been killed.

GEEST *ST. LUCIA* CONTAINER SHIP

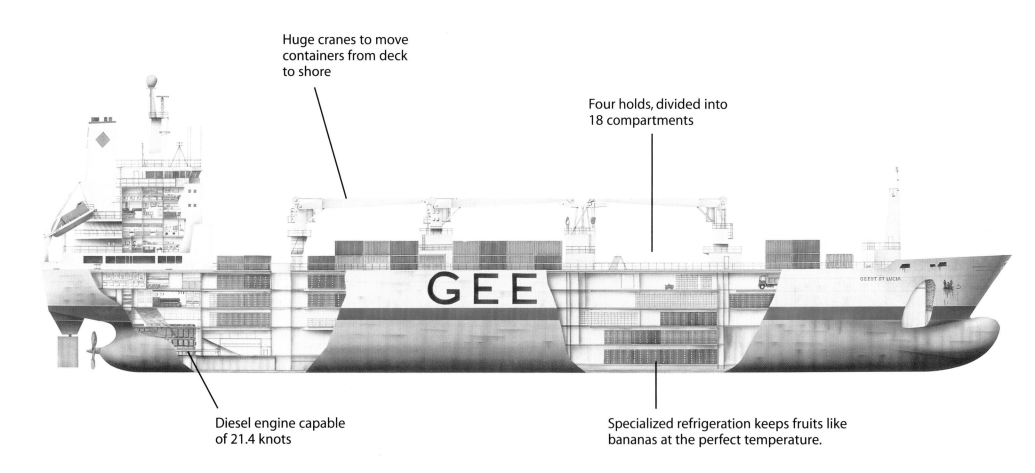

Huge cranes to move containers from deck to shore

Four holds, divided into 18 compartments

Diesel engine capable of 21.4 knots

Specialized refrigeration keeps fruits like bananas at the perfect temperature.

It takes time to unload individual boxes and sacks of goods from trucks or trains and then load them onto a ship, which is why container ships were designed. These huge vessels have warehouse-style cargo holds. Goods arrive in specially built containers by road or rail and the whole container is lifted by crane onto the ship. Container ships like the *St. Lucia* are designed specially for transporting exotic fruit from the Caribbean and so are equipped with four separate holds and refrigeration units.

Did You Know?

The *St. Lucia's* navigational computer is so sophisticated that, if necessary, the entire ship could be piloted by one person.

Exotic Fruits Direct from the Tropics!

ABOVE: The arrival of refrigerated container ships has allowed people all over the world to eat foods that they would normally never have the opportunity to try.

Keeping Food Fresh

Traditional container ships can carry a range of goods very effectively, but fruit and vegetables need special care to ensure that they don't spoil during the journey. At ordinary temperatures, bacteria would soon begin to rot food, but if the food is chilled, the process can be slowed down. This method of food preservation was pioneered by Clarence Birdseye, who noticed during a hunting trip that fish that were frozen almost immediately after being caught were still just as tasty when thawed. It's this principle of refrigeration that allows container ships to transport food and vegetables around the globe.

The *St. Lucia* and her sister ship, the *Dominica*, were designed to cope with the huge rise in demand for exotic fruit and vegetables from the Caribbean over the last decade. They're owned by Geest plc, which has built its business by selling fresh and prepared foods, so the quality of its goods is an important consideration. Like many specialized container ships, the *St. Lucia's* vast cargo hold contains refrigeration units, which can keep goods either chilled or frozen. There's also space on deck for "reefer" containers, which have built-in refrigeration units that run off the ship's electrical systems.

163

THE TURTLE

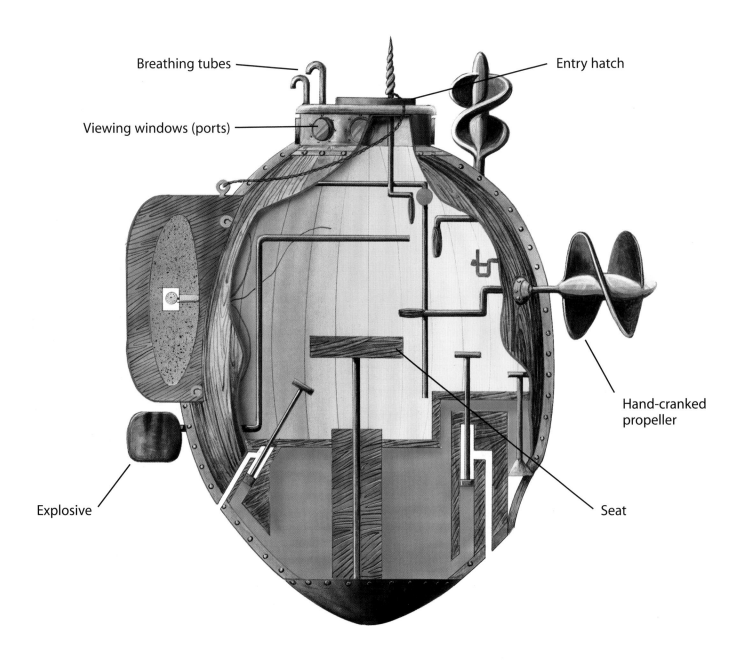

Breathing tubes

Entry hatch

Viewing windows (ports)

Hand-cranked propeller

Explosive

Seat

Made of wood, with no engine, and with space inside for a crew of just one member, *The Turtle* looks more like a toy than a serious piece of military hardware. Despite her curious appearance, this strange, egglike craft has an important place in the record books. Piloted by Sergeant Ezra Lee in New York Harbor in 1776, *The Turtle* was the first submarine ever to be used for underwater warfare.

Did You Know?

In 1190, a German poet wrote about a hero called Morolf, who made a diving boat out of leather to hide at the bottom of the ocean.

Underwater Experiments

Since the time of Alexander the Great, around 300 B.C., military thinkers have looked for practical ways to wage war at sea, undetected by the enemy. Numerous accounts of strange and wonderful craft survive, but it wasn't until the 1500s that the inventor and artist Leonardo da Vinci (see page 143) claimed to have actually designed a practical underwater machine. However, he refused to reveal details of his work, saying that he did not trust "the evil nature of men who practice assassination at the bottom of the sea." The world had to wait until 1626 for the first practical "submersible" to be demonstrated. Designed by Cornelius von Drebble, who was an inventor at the Court of King James I of England, this early "sub" looked like an upside-down rowing boat. In fact, this is almost exactly was it was! Drebble simply put a "lid" on a large fishing boat, and covered the whole device with grease to make it waterproof. Remarkably, he even had 12 oarsmen inside to row the boat along! His device may have sounded crazy, but he succeeded in sailing it 12 feet below the River Thames—making it the first ever tried and tested submarine.

HOLLAND VI

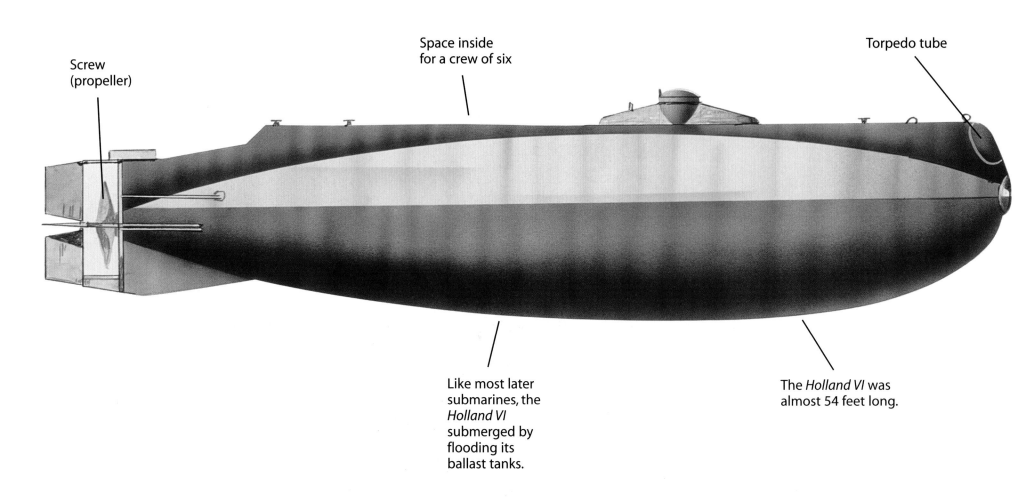

Screw
(propeller)

Space inside
for a crew of six

Torpedo tube

Like most later
submarines, the
Holland VI
submerged by
flooding its
ballast tanks.

The *Holland VI* was
almost 54 feet long.

The *Holland VI,* named after her inventor J.P. Holland, was the American navy's first submarine. Bought in 1900, this incredible craft was driven by a gas engine and could reach 8 knots, which was an impressive speed for the time. It was even equipped with three torpedoes! Holland's understanding of underwater propulsion was so advanced that, even today, modern submariners would recognize much of the design and layout of this cutting-edge craft.

Did You Know?

During the American Civil War a Confederate submarine, the *Hunley,* became the first submarine to sink a ship in wartime.

Revolutionary Ideas!

BELOW: John Philip Holland, whose first submarine, the *Fenian Ram,* was financed by Irish nationalists, saw the submarine as the ideal "hit and run" terror weapon against the British navy.

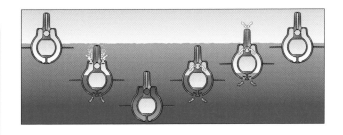

What Is Buoyancy?

Place an object in water and it will sink until it has "displaced" (pushed away) an amount of water equal to its own weight, or density. Some objects have a negative buoyancy. They are more dense than water, and will always sink. Objects with a positive buoyancy will float. This picture shows how submarines use the principle of buoyancy to sink and resurface. In the first, left-hand submarine, ballast tanks have been filled with air, giving the craft full buoyancy. To sink, valves on these tanks are opened. Water from outside rushes into the ballast tanks, pushing out the air, and the submarine then starts to sink. A craft like the *Holland* will "displace" 76 tons of water when submerged. To resurface, this process is reversed. The valves are reopened and air, under pressure, is blown into the ballast tanks. This forces the water out, eventually reestablishing positive buoyancy.

TYPE VII U-BOAT

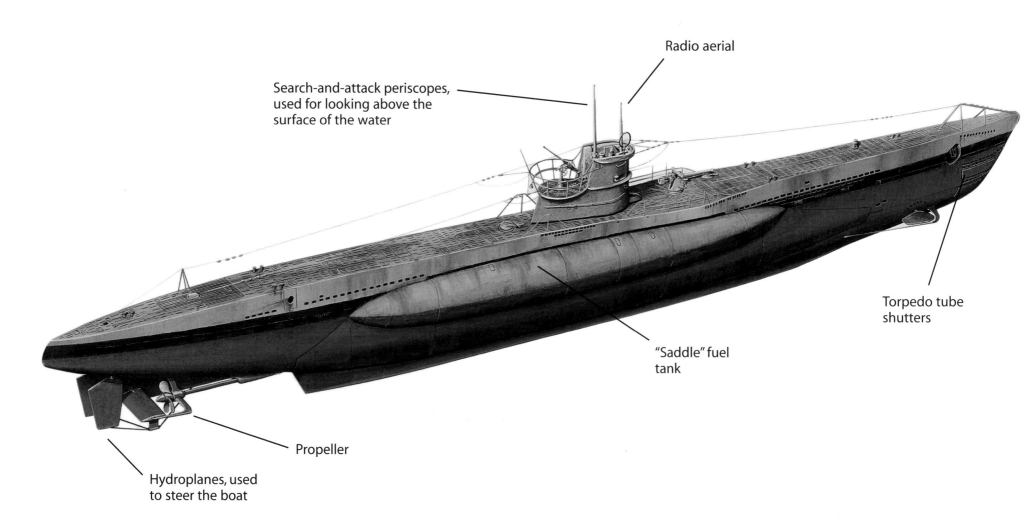

Search-and-attack periscopes, used for looking above the surface of the water

Radio aerial

Torpedo tube shutters

"Saddle" fuel tank

Propeller

Hydroplanes, used to steer the boat

During World War II, German submarines, called *Untersee Boote,* or U-boats, sank thousands of merchant ships. In the first seven months of the conflict, at least five ships were sunk by every U-boat. These hidden hunters traveled in "Wolf Packs" of up to 40 submarines, and any ship in the Atlantic was their prey. Until the introduction of sonar made them easier to detect, U-boats were the masters of the oceans.

Definitions

sonar: (Meaning Sound, Navigation, and Ranging.) Method of using sound waves to locate objects, in a similar way to radar.

Did You Know?

The life of a submariner was extremely dangerous. Out of almost 50,000 men who served aboard U-boats, 63 percent lost their lives.

Turning Fuel into Power

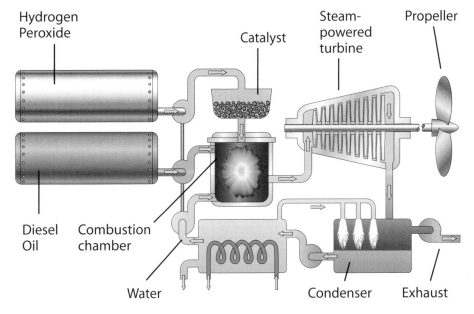

Hydrogen Peroxide

Catalyst

Steam-powered turbine

Propeller

Diesel Oil

Combustion chamber

Water

Condenser

Exhaust

ABOVE: U-boats were cramped and uncomfortable places.

Energy can't be created or destroyed, but it can be changed from one form into another. For example, in a traditional car engine, gas and air are mixed inside the cylinder and then a spark is used to cause the mixture to burn ("combust"). Burning releases the energy that is stored in the fuel as mechanical energy. This mechanical energy powers the engine. U-boats used a revolutionary new type of engine called a Walther engine. This diagram shows how the Walther engine worked. Concentrated hydrogen peroxide, called Ingolin, is passed over a chemical catalyst, which causes it to give off oxygen. This oxygen is burned with diesel oil inside the combustion chamber. The heat of combustion turns the water, which is being pumped into the chamber, into steam. This makes the blades of the turbine spin. The Walther engine was designed to be both powerful and "clean." The heat of exhaust fumes can be detected by an enemy, so a condenser is used to cool the exhaust gases before they leave the submarine.

S.S.G.N. *KURSK* NUCLEAR SUBMARINE

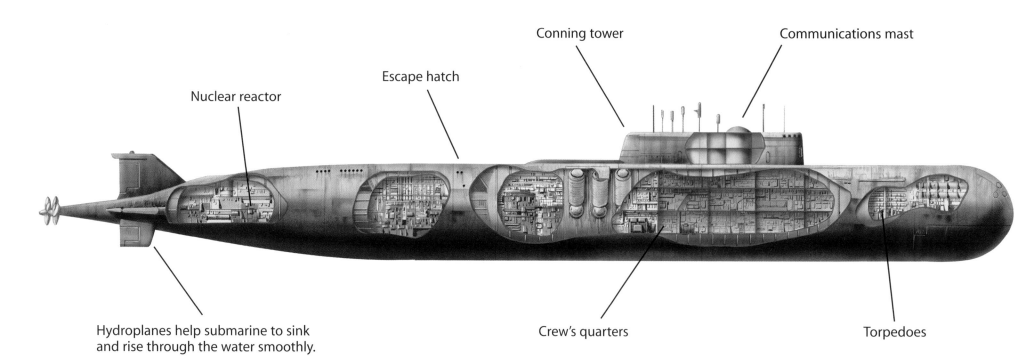

Conning tower

Communications mast

Escape hatch

Nuclear reactor

Hydroplanes help submarine to sink and rise through the water smoothly.

Crew's quarters

Torpedoes

In size, weight, and power, the *Kursk* was an incredible example of submarine design and engineering brilliance. This titanic submarine measured 508 feet, which is over twice the length of a Boeing 747. Equipped with the latest satellite surveillance equipment and 24 supersonic cruise missiles, the *Kursk* was built to hunt and sink aircraft carriers. Sadly, like the *Titanic*, she will be forever remembered for the terrible tragedy that happened to her and her crew when the submarine sank in the Barents Sea in August 2000.

Did You Know?

All submariners have to undertake escape training throughout their careers.

Search and Rescue

BELOW: This Deep Sea Rescue Vehicle (D.S.R.V.) is designed to be attached to the hull of disabled submarines. It can dive to a depth of 2000 feet.

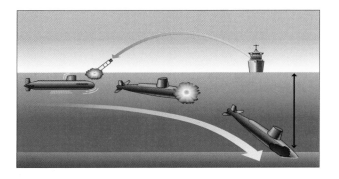

The Story of the *Kursk*

In August 2000, 118 submariners lost their lives when the Russian submarine *Kursk* was sunk in the Barents Sea. A call for help went out, and rescue ships such as the British Royal Navy's LR5 were sent to the region. There seemed every reason to hope that some of the crew would be found alive. Soon, however, it was discovered that the accident had happened many days before the Russian authorities asked for help. This has been seen by some as proof that the tragedy was caused by a missile test gone wrong, as illustrated above. The wreck of the *Kursk* has since been raised and the hull shows signs of a collision, so the *Kursk* may have been sunk by a practice torpedo. Tragically, the accident damaged both the forward escape hatch and internal escape capsule. By the time the rescuers arrived, it was already too late to save any lives.

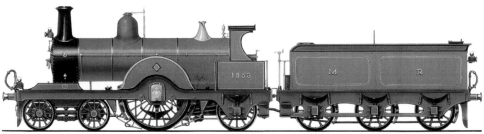

CHAPTER NINE

Steam Locomotives

For more than a century after the invention of the steam locomotive, these impressive machines remained not just the fastest way to travel, but the most glamorous too.

Railroads existed long before locomotives were invented. Simple iron tracks—"railroads"—had been used to guide horse-drawn coal trucks in and out of mines since the 1500s. Steam engines arrived about 200 years later and soon replaced the horse as a more efficient way of moving heavy loads. It wasn't until 1804 that a Cornish mining engineer, Richard Trevithick, decided to use the same technology to transport people. Trevithick's idea was one of those brilliant flashes of genius that change the world. Soon, steam locomotives were roaring across the countryside, transporting passengers across Europe, Africa, Asia, and the Americas.

STEPHENSON 0-2-2 *NORTHUMBRIAN*

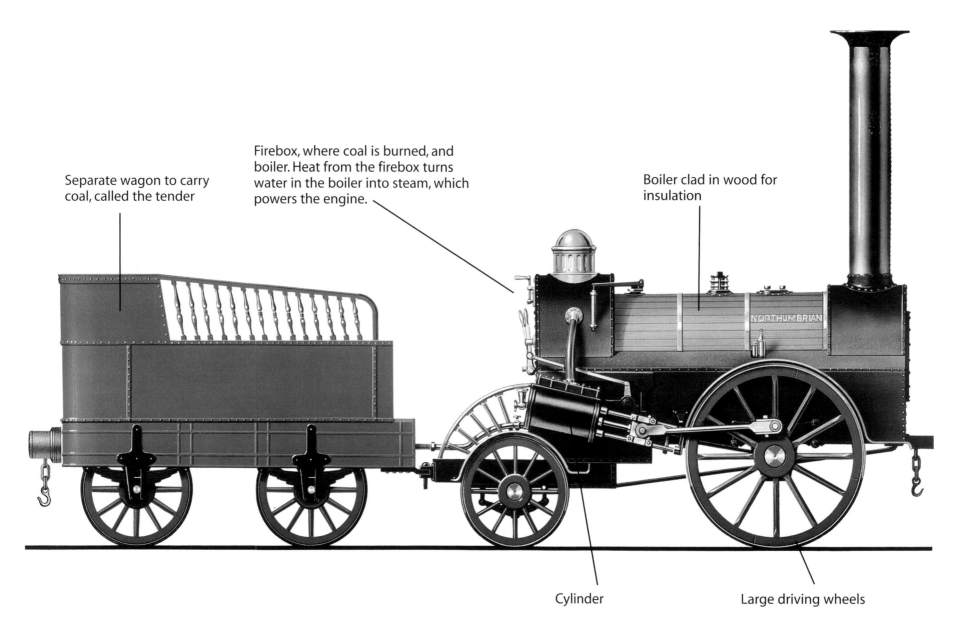

Separate wagon to carry coal, called the tender

Firebox, where coal is burned, and boiler. Heat from the firebox turns water in the boiler into steam, which powers the engine.

Boiler clad in wood for insulation

Cylinder

Large driving wheels

Robert and George Stephenson, a father-and-son team, were the creative force behind the successful *Rocket* locomotive. *Northumbrian*, which was built in 1830, was a larger version of *Rocket* and was capable of a top speed of 36 mph. At the time, it was believed that people wouldn't be able to breathe at speeds over 20 mph!

• •

Definitions
locomotive: Engine driven by steam, diesel, or electric, used to pull carriages on a railroad. (A "train" is the engine plus carriages.)

• •

Did You Know?

The first victim of a train accident was hit and killed by Stephenson's *Rocket*.

A Pioneering Invention

ABOVE: A nineteenth-century illustration of Stephenson's *Rocket*.

The Rainhill Trials

Rocket is one of the most famous locomotives in railroad history. In 1829, the Liverpool and Manchester Company was looking for engines to use on its new railroad, and decided to invite the country's best engineers to enter a competition. The only rules were that the engines had to weigh less than six tons, have sprung wheels, cost no more than £500 to build, and be able to reach a speed of 10 mph. Over 10,000 people turned up to watch the trials of five very different engines. One, the

Cycloped, was powered by a horse walking on a treadmill! The crowd's favorite, *Novelty*, was the smallest locomotive and stunned onlookers by reaching 28 mph. Unfortunately, its boiler blew up and it had to be withdrawn from the competition. Stephenson's *Rocket*, pictured above, performed well over the range of tests, averaging 29 mph unloaded, and 12 mph pulling wagons. Stephenson won the £500 prize and a contract to produce locomotives, which made his fortune and set the pattern for future locomotive design.

NORRIS 4-2-0 *LAFAYETTE*

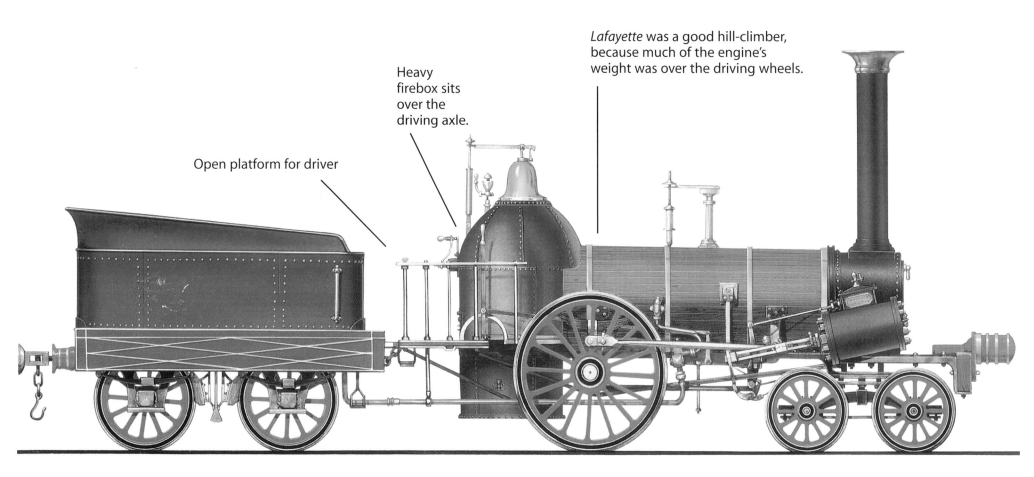

Lafayette was a good hill-climber, because much of the engine's weight was over the driving wheels.

Heavy firebox sits over the driving axle.

Open platform for driver

The Norris 4-2-0 was built in 1837 as a specialized hill-climber. *Lafayette* was the first of eight examples. Her unusual design depended on placing more weight than was usual over the locomotive's large driving wheels. This gave the locomotive greater grip. *Lafayette* brought her designer, William Norris, fame and fortune and he went on to build locomotives for 27 U.S. railroads as well as countries as far afield as Austria, Italy, and Cuba.

Did You Know?

The world's first public railroad to use steam-powered locomotives to pull carriages carrying passengers was the Stockton and Darlington Railway in northeast England. It was opened in 1825 and covered 26 miles.

Nation Building

It's no exaggeration to say that in many countries, the arrival of the railroads changed life forever. In America, rail was a vital part of the process of nation-building, as it was rail travel that opened up the West to new settlers. During the nineteenth century, about 253,000 miles of track was laid. Most of this backbreaking work was done by Chinese workers, who were brought in from Asia to do the job. Their experience and skill in completing similar work in China made them an ideal workforce. By 1868, more than two-thirds of the 4,000 rail workers were Chinese. Many of the rest were Irish. The work they did was often very dangerous. Thousands were injured, many died, and the average wage was just $28 a month. In 1999, representative John Doolittle paid tribute to the amazing contribution that these Chinese workers made. Speaking in the House of Representatives, he said: "Without the efforts of the Chinese workers in the building of America's railroads, our development and progress as a nation would have been delayed by years. Their toil in severe weather, cruel working conditions, and for meager wages cannot be underappreciated. My sentiments and thanks go out to the entire Chinese-American community for its ancestors' contribution to the building of this great nation."

Chinese Laborers

ABOVE: Chinese laborers pictured during the building of the Northern Pacific Railroad in western Montana, USA.

AMERICAN TYPE 4-4-0

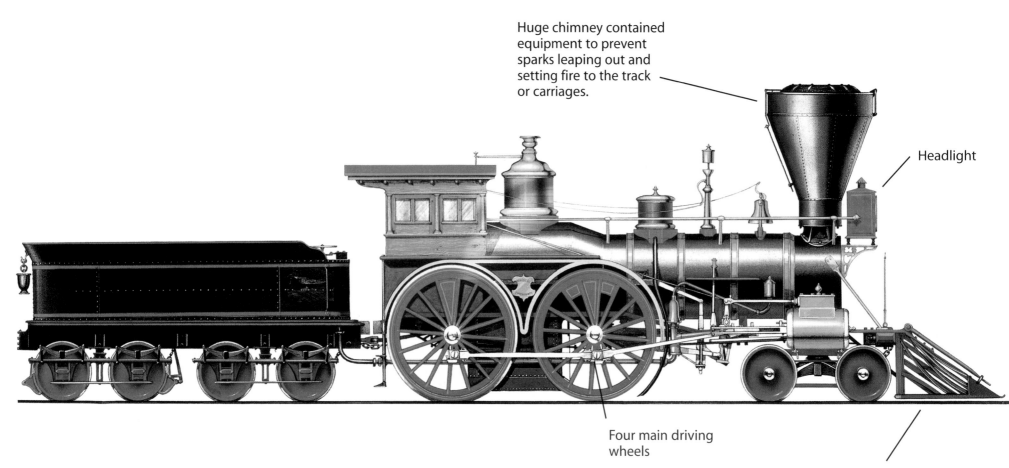

Huge chimney contained equipment to prevent sparks leaping out and setting fire to the track or carriages.

Headlight

Four main driving wheels

Pilot, or "cow-catcher." This is used to clear the track of obstructions.

America quickly fell in love with train travel, which offered a cheap and fast way of covering the huge distances between her nation's towns and cities. By the 1830s, three big names dominated the rapidly growing home-built industry: Baldwin, Norris, and Rogers. The American Type 4-4-0 shown here was built in 1855 by the Rogers Locomotive Works in New Jersey, and is now considered a classic. This sleek, powerful "loco" remained King of the Railroads for almost 50 years.

Did You Know?

The first American-built locomotive, *Best Friend of Charleston,* was made only a year after Stephenson's *Rocket* won the Rainhill Trials.

Star Acts

This still is from the well-known 1926 film *The General,* starring Buster Keaton. The film is a comedy based on a true story about a Confederate locomotive driver who had his train stolen by Union soldiers. The locomotive featured was an American Type 4-4-0. The story was so famous that Disney made another version of the tale, called *The Great Locomotive Chase,* in 1956.

Famous Names

The railroad world is full of famous names, but some have become so celebrated that the very mention of them is enough to conjure up images of luxury and elegance. When the crime writer Agatha Christie set one of her murder mysteries aboard the Venice–Simplon *Orient Express,* she made the luxury European train world famous. In America, the *20th Century Limited*, which ran from Chicago to New York, between 1902 and 1967, was just as stylish. Its deluxe sleeping cars, luxury fittings, and spectacular food very quickly made it a favorite with a host of Hollywood stars, who regularly traveled on her. However, at the top of the list must be South Africa's *Blue Train*. This luxury service has been running since 1939 and every suite on board boasts its own TV and private phone.

STIRLING 8-FOOT SINGLE 4-2-2

The Stirling singles were built for the
Great Northern Railway to run between
London and York.

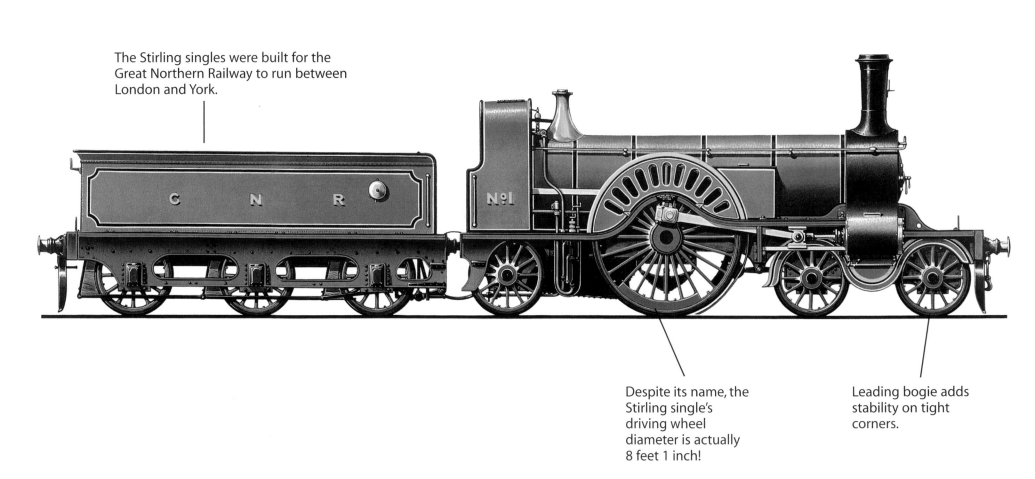

Despite its name, the
Stirling single's
driving wheel
diameter is actually
8 feet 1 inch!

Leading bogie adds
stability on tight
corners.

The 1880s are often called the "Golden Age of Steam" and, as far as many loco-enthusiasts are concerned, the most beautiful engines were built during this time. These engines weren't just handsome, they were well-designed, powerful, and built to last. Locomotives like the Stirling single were made between 1870 and 1895, but continued to be used right up until 1919, becoming a well-known feature of the British countryside.

- -

Definitions
bogie: Also called a pony truck. This is a set of wheels at the front of the train that adds stability.

- -

Did You Know?

The fastest regular passenger steam locomotive was *The Cheltenham Flyer,* which was operated by Britain's Great Western Railway in the 1930s.

Record-Breakers

During the 1890s, fierce competition erupted between Britain's east and west coast rail companies. The argument was about who could complete the journey between London and Edinburgh the fastest. Finally, on August 20, 1895, one of Patrick Stirling's singles was attached to an East Coast Express and allowed to run flat out along the route. The resulting time of 6 hours 19 minutes was a record, and it stood unbeaten until 1935. In 1904, race fever broke out again, and this time the Great Western Railway set a record with the locomotive *The Cheltenham Flyer.* By the 1930s, the fight was on again. For 20 years, the east and west coast companies had agreed not to compete with each other on journey times. However, the increasing popularity of car travel was threatening both companies with financial ruin. If they could prove that trains were faster than cars, there was money to be made. Locomotive design had changed very little in the previous 50 years, and the basic technology being used was the same. What was different was the way the locomotives looked, thanks to a new idea called streamlining. Over the next few years these streamlined locos broke record after record until finally, in 1938, the A4 Pacific Mallard made a top speed of 126 mph. This record has never been beaten by a steam train.

JOHNSON MIDLAND SINGLE 4-2-2

The dome contained safety valves.

Midland singles were capable of speeds of up to 90 mph.

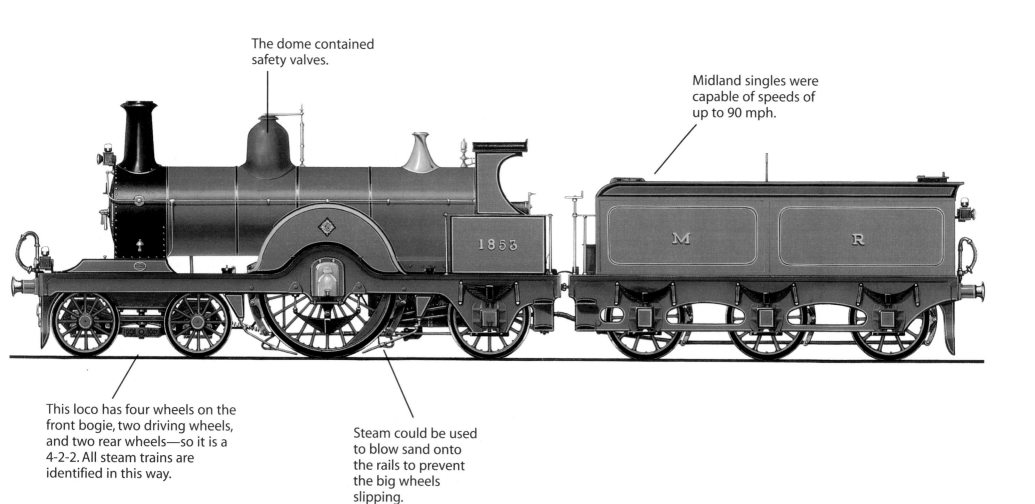

1853

M   R

This loco has four wheels on the front bogie, two driving wheels, and two rear wheels—so it is a 4-2-2. All steam trains are identified in this way.

Steam could be used to blow sand onto the rails to prevent the big wheels slipping.

Samuel Waite Johnson is one of the lesser-known names in locomotive design. Born in 1831, Johnson spent his entire working life in the railroad business, yet he produced very few engine designs. The reason was simple: Although he introduced many innovations during his time with the Derby and Midland Railway, he rarely took sole credit for his ideas. Instead he preferred to encourage others, and the success of his beautifully streamlined singles was all about good teamwork.

Did You Know?

Johnson's singles were nicknamed "Midland Spinners" because of their single driving axle.

Railroad Time

In the 1800s, every town had its own "local" time, based on the position of the sun in the sky. Even in a small country like Britain, there's a half-hour difference between the time that the sun rises in the east of the country and when it rises in the west. These differences in "local time" were not important until the first railroads were built, when an accurate way of telling the time became essential. After all, how could timetables be set without a standardized system of timekeeping? Between 1840 and 1880, Britain's railroads struggled with the problem. Some adopted "London" time; others continued to use local time. Many used both systems; station clocks had two minute hands, showing both times! Not surprisingly, timetables were confusing. Traveling west, for example, would always take longer than doing the same journey east! Then, in 1880, the British government set a standard time across the country. In 1884, to make traveling between countries easier, standard World Time Zones were established. This divided the world into 24 zones. World time zones are a set number of hours behind or ahead of GMT, or Greenwich Mean Time, named after the location of the Royal Observatory in Greenwich, England.

CLAUD HAMILTON CLASS 4-4-0

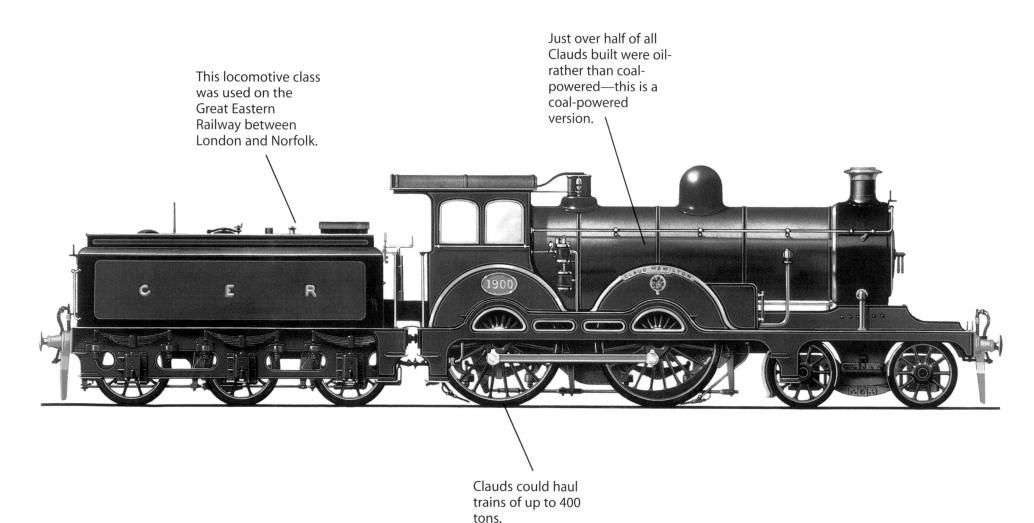

This locomotive class was used on the Great Eastern Railway between London and Norfolk.

Just over half of all Clauds built were oil- rather than coal- powered—this is a coal-powered version.

Clauds could haul trains of up to 400 tons.

The history of this grand-looking locomotive stretches across an incredible 60 years. Between 1900 and 1911, 101 of these powerful machines were built but their huge pulling power meant that they remained in use on passenger expresses until the end of World War II, and as freight carriers right up until the start of the swinging 1960s.

Did You Know?

The Claud Hamilton locomotive was named after the Chairman of Britain's Great Eastern Railway.

Inside the Boiler

ABOVE: A steam train's boiler contains a number of small pipes to provide a large surface area.

How Steam Power Works

If you've ever seen how the lid on a kettle lifts slightly when the kettle starts to boil, you've seen steam power at work. The idea of using this process to create movement was first demonstrated by a scientist called Hero, who lived in Egypt around A.D. 60. Hero's "engine" was an arrangement of pipes from a container of water to a small globe. When the water in the container boiled, the steam traveled through the pipes and made the globe spin. It wasn't until the late 1700s that engineers like James Watt and Richard Trevithick (see pages 174–175) designed and built the first true steam engines, but the principles remain the same as in Hero's simple toy. In a locomotive, fuel is burned in the firebox. The heat is taken through pipes into the boiler, which causes the water stored there to boil. As the water changes into steam, it expands. The pressure created by the steam drives pistons that are attached to piston rods. These rods move the driving wheels. Expanding gases can be dangerous, as they put the boiler under huge pressure. In a badly built boiler, this pressure will split the metal seams (called gaskets) of the engine apart. This is called "blowing a gasket," an expression still used today for someone in an uncontrollable rage.

UNION PACIFIC CLASS FEF-2 4-8-4

A huge trailing truck with 12 wheels was necessary to provide the firebox with enough coal.

The FEF-2 was 114 feet long.

The huge FEF-2s could haul 1000 tons at 100 mph.

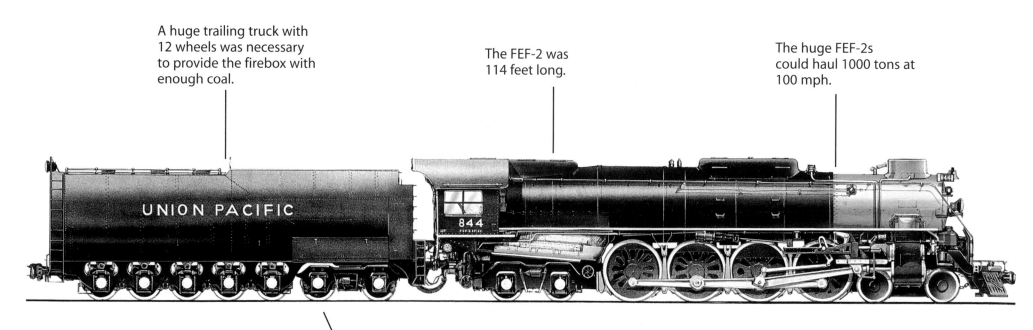

The FEF was first used on passenger trains by the New York Central Railroad in 1927.

From the beginning of train travel, the designer's problem has always been how to get the locomotive to pull more weight without any loss of speed or control. Heavier trains need bigger, more powerful engines and more axles to spread the weight evenly over the tracks. With this in mind, the massive 405-ton Union Pacific FEF (Four-Eight-Four) has eight driving wheels and a huge boiler with a diameter of 7 feet 6 inches.

Dangerous But Free

ABOVE: Men hitch a ride to southern California on the Union Pacific Railroad in 1934.

Hitching a Ride

Between the 1880s and the 1940s, hoboes were a regular sight on America's railroads. For decades, these "tramps of the tracks" have been celebrated in movies and in songs, and even today the wandering, uncluttered lifestyle of the hobo seems romantic. Yet, for hoboes, life could be tough. Many of those who ended up traveling the railroads didn't choose to be wanderers. They'd simply found themselves homeless and unemployed at the end of the American Civil War. For people like this, the railroads were a godsend. They offered them an ideal way of traveling from job to job and, for anyone brave enough to "hitch a ride" on one of the passing goods trains, travel was free. The word *hobo* comes from the term "hoe-boy" and, starting in June every year, thousands of hoboes would follow the harvest, ending up in North Dakota by August. To those who lived in the cities, hoboes were just unemployed "drifters," but farms and logging and mining companies depended on this mobile and flexible workforce. Until the arrival of cheap and reliable machinery, hoboes were the powerhouses of businesses up and down the Midwest.

INDIAN CLASS YP 4-6-2

"Elephant-ear" smoke deflectors keep smoke away from the engine driver's line of vision.

The YP Class 4-6-2 was the most common passenger locomotive in India after independence.

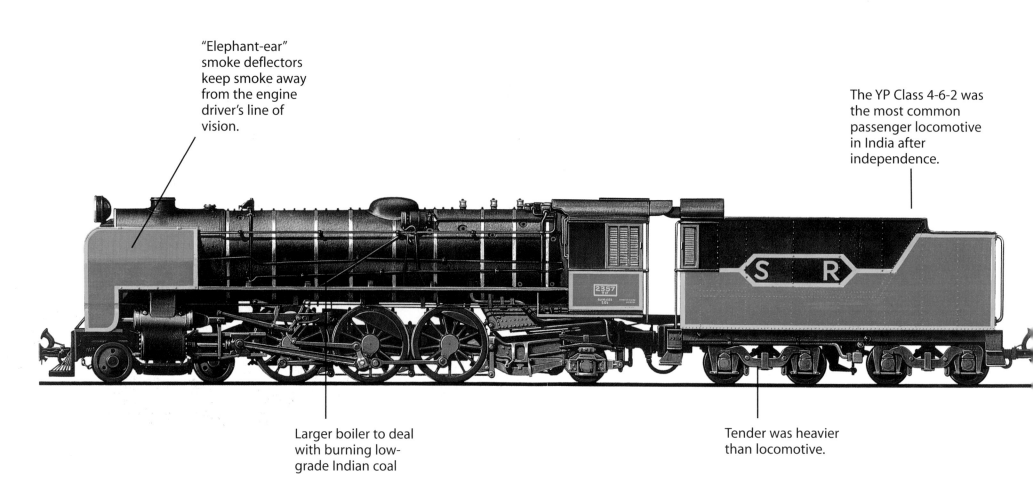

Larger boiler to deal with burning low-grade Indian coal

Tender was heavier than locomotive.

Much of India's railroads were built before there was a standard gauge (size) for railroad tracks. Tracks were laid depending on the distance between a loco's wheels. When gauges became standardized, old tracks either had to be replaced or new trains adapted to run on them. After independence, India decided to tackle this problem by standardizing its new locomotives. The YP was the first of the new breed, designed to run on the new metric Y gauge rails.

Did You Know?

The YPs were among the very last steam locomotives built for passenger services.

Indian Railroads

The first commercial passenger train journey in India took place on April 16, 1853. The train, containing 14 carriages and pulled by three locomotives (the Sindh, Sultan, and Sahib), left Bombay after receiving a 21-gun salute, which heralded the start of India's great railroad age. At first, the development of India's rail network was controlled by the British, who had ruled India since 1757. The British felt that it was vital to have some way of uniting such a huge nation. So, a program of rail building was begun, which took trains across the country from busy commercial ports such as Madras to isolated villages high up in the spectacular snow-topped Himalayan mountains. Since independence in the 1950s, the Indian government has continued to develop this vital service. New underground routes

have been added to the system in major cities like Calcutta. And in some of the more popular tourist regions, steam locomotives continue to offer a touch of old-style luxury. The result is the largest rail system in the world.

This covers an amazing 66,484 miles and carries over 11 million passengers a day. Some routes are so popular that passengers even cling on to the outside of the carriages!

INDEX

PICTURE CREDITS

All photographs and illustrations courtesy Art-Tech/Aerospace except:

Action Plus: 47
Roy Bacon: 20
Roland Brown: 11r, 21
Cody Images: 9l, 31 (both), 33, 81r, 88c, 98, 99 (Case), 101l, 131r, 159, 181 (D. Burrows), 185 (D. Burrows)
Corbis Images: 37 (both), 41, 55, 57, 75t, 105r, 137, 143l, 153, 155, 157, 161 (both), 163, 175 (both), 177, 179, 183, 187, 189
De Agostini: 6c, 14, 16, 166
Fondation De L'Automobile Marius Berliet, Lyon, France: 82

Getty Images: 121br
The Kobal Collection: 77
Lincolnshire County Archives/Wordsworth Holdings PLC: 104, 105l
Lister Cars Limited: 45l
Tony Matthews: 28bl, 28br (Lola Ford), 28tr (DH Enterprises), 32, 38 (Lola Ford), 44 (DH Enterprises), 46
Marshall Cavendish: 90, 92
National Motor Museum: 9r, 73r
QA Photos Ltd: 97

Quadrant Picture Library: 79
Royal Navy Submarine Museum: 165, 167l, 171l
SDV: 169r
Stephen Seymour: 172 (all), 174, 176, 178, 180, 182, 184, 186
Sutton Motorsport Images: 35, 39, 43r, 45
Mike Schram: 75b
John Tipler: 28tl, 40, 42
Mick Walker: 6tl, 12, 17, 25 (both)
Michael Williams: 50br (Caterpillar), 59, 61r, 63, 65, 66 (Caterpillar), 67 (Caterpillar), 69l (Claas), 69r, 83l
Wylde Parnell/WBM: 95

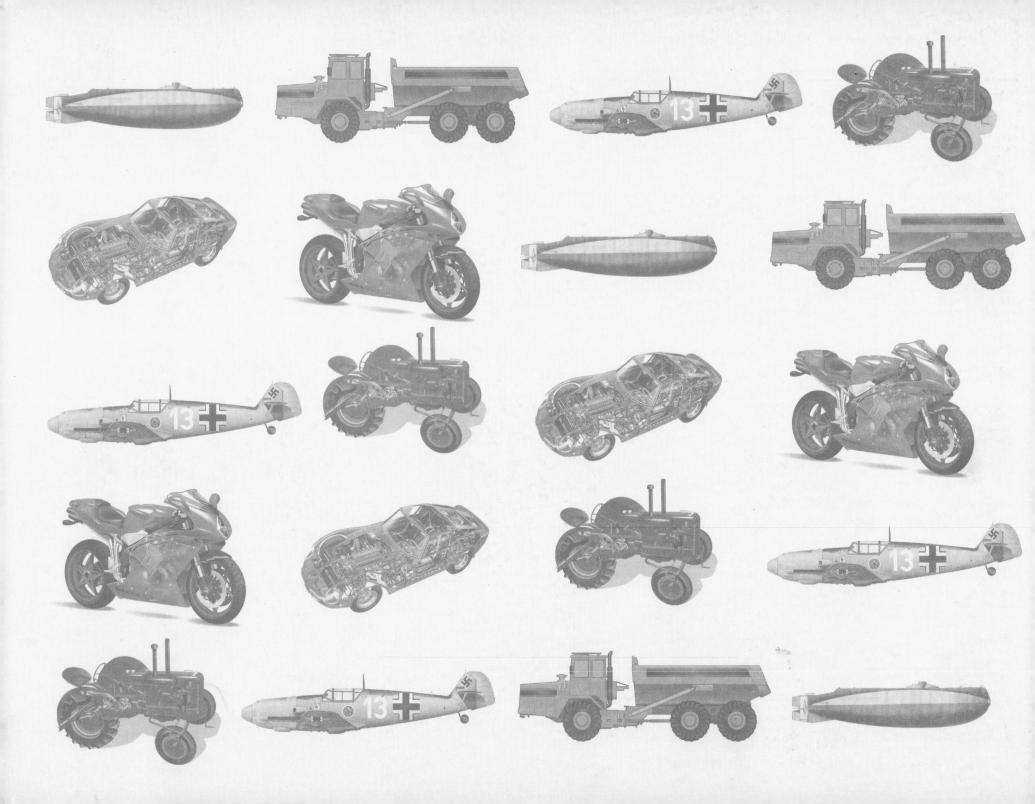